A Bundle of Sticks

A Memoir

by Judy Darby

'A family is like a bundle of sticks: if one breaks away the whole bundle disintegrates.'

Published by New Generation Publishing in 2016

Copyright © Judy Darby 2016

First Edition

The author asserts the moral right under the Copyright, Designs and Patents Act 1988 to be identified as the author of this work.

All Rights reserved. No part of this publication may be reproduced, stored in a retrieval system or transmitted, in any form or by any means without the prior consent of the author, nor be otherwise circulated in any form of binding or cover other than that which it is published and without a similar condition being imposed on the subsequent purchaser.

www.newgeneration-publishing.com

New Generation Publishing

For Shirley and Tony, with gratitude and love

Acknowledgements

There are many people I am indebted to for their encouragement and support. Firstly, my brother, Tony, who wished me to write this account, but who did not live long enough to see its completion.

Love and appreciation to my dear sister, Shirley, who supplied infinite memories and knowledge. Transatlantic calls, long into the night, provided much of the content of this story.

Julie Wheelwright, at City University, is a superlative teacher, and I gained tremendously from my MA course under her guidance. I am immensely grateful to her for all her help with early drafts, and also to Sarah Bakewell, another excellent and gifted teacher. Thanks, also, to my fellow students, who supported and advised, especially Maria and Caitlin.

Thank you to Elspeth Sinclair, for all her help and encouragement.

My wonderful friend, Val Goodyear, unstintingly gave her time, wisdom and knowledge at all stages, and her belief in this project sustained me throughout.

I thank my excellent friends Daphne Adam and Sheila Jones for their warmth and faith.

My children have supported me in ways they might not envisage, and have been a constant source of strength and love throughout all my endeavours.

Many thanks to Penny and Hannah for immediate response and help with word processing problems, and to them and David for tolerance and help with my computer illiteracy.

A huge thank you to Sally Cline, my Gold Dust mentor, who always believed when I did not. Her professional expertise has rescued me from many an error, and she has revolutionised my approach to writing over many mugs of coffee in the British Library.

To Clinical Hypnotherapist, David Samson, I offer heartfelt gratitude for his wisdom, brilliance and patience in giving me insight, and a new confidence and self-belief. Without him I would not have got this far.

And finally, to my wonderful sister, the other Judy, who wrote the epilogue to this book. I am thankful that you found us, and cherish our friendship.

A Bundle of Sticks

Contents

Chapter 1: Revelation 1

Chapter 2: 322 Luton Road 7

Chapter 3: My Grandparents 27

Chapter 4: Education and Experience................................. 39

Chapter 5: Abortion and Adoption 63

Chapter 6: Felpham 82

Chapter 7: On the Move 103

Chapter 8: Musical Festivals 121

Chapter 9: Misrule 129

Chapter 10: Mourning and Marriage 139

Chapter 11: Dark Days 153

Chapter 12: Running Away 172

Chapter 13: Breaking Point 187

Chapter 14: Aftermath 197

Chapter 15: Meeting 200

Epilogue.. 204

The Children - taken for Dad's 50th birthday 1956
From left to right back row: Roger, Shirley, Tony
From left to right front row: Judy, Jill, Valerie, Roy

Chapter 1: Revelation

Friday, November 17th, 1961

Coincidences and the month of November can be grim.

I stood in the Head teacher's room. I was only there because my brother, Tony, had sent me to school, and told me exactly what to say. At that time I obeyed him unquestioningly. My mother had died the night before and we had sat up all night talking, but Tony decided that everything should be as normal. Tony never made concessions to tiredness: he was like our father. At school, with numb politeness I told Mrs. Evans what had happened. She was a comfortable-looking woman, approaching sixty, her grandmotherly air hiding a sharp intellect. When occasion demanded she could be frightening.

Today her concern was warm, genuine and unwanted. She touched my arm gently, and I flinched. In the house where I grew up, no one had touched me since infancy, except in anger. We didn't hug or kiss, and I was embarrassed by those who did.

'Go home, Judith dear,' urged the kindly Head. 'I'm sure there's a great deal to do and arrange.' I'm sure there was, but it was all in hands more competent than mine. Tony had told me to go to school, and I was grateful for the illusion of normality.

I turned away from the Head's room and made my way down the corridor. Over a thousand girls were on the move, and yet no one spoke. The school rules were uncompromising, and silence in the corridor was one of them. Feet marched in straight lines round a one-way system, rubber and leather slapping the floor in unison. As a prefect I could walk against the traffic: it was easy as the line of navy tunics kept to one side.

I suddenly spotted a young girl coming towards me among a line of fourth years. She had brown, wavy hair like mine, but bouncier, thicker, prettier. She had dark, sensitive eyes, a face with a ready smile. She was taller than I was, but three years younger, and I thought that she looked at ease with herself and the world.

Prefects sat with classes when teachers were absent, but I had never overseen this young girl's class. As I gave out the set work, making the usual comments about doing it in silence, I would, however, scan the room, just in case.

Now I looked straight at her, and she looked back without even registering my presence. I was just another prefect. The first emotion to pierce my numbness crept over me as silent panic set in. The thought was unbidden, unwelcome: that girl's mother died last night, and she doesn't know.

Thursday, June 5th, 1953

I woke up with a tight feeling in my chest. But why? I struggled to remember. Beyond the uncurtained window there was no hint of malice in the sky. It was Coronation year, a time of national and street celebration, and although Elizabeth had formally accepted her destiny three days ago, in the pouring rain, the weather had now relented.

Beside me, stretched out diagonally across the bed we shared, my older sister, Jill, did not stir. Suddenly I remembered why I was troubled: that evening we were competing in the annual Dunstable Musical Festival, a spectacularly ambitious programme, against individual candidates from all over the county. We couldn't play musical instruments, but our mother had entered us in the poetry sections for our different age groups. There was no way we would dare to refuse.

I thought of my words:
A ship sails up to Bideford, upon a western breeze…

I pushed away the grey army blankets without disturbing Jill, and tiptoed with bare feet, down the stairs. In the kitchen my mother, Violet, was banging dishes around, her forehead creased, her lips a tight, narrow strip. I sidled into the room, anxious not to offend.

'Is there anything I can do, Mum?'

She looked up, dark curls tangled, but dominant, determined and as always, angry. 'Don't let me down, tonight. I've spent weeks rehearsing you for this. You'll be up against all those posh competitors who have paid to be coached.'

Anxiety hung over her like a cowl.

Jill appeared in the doorway, silent and watchful. Our mother swung round. 'And that goes for you, too.'

Jill nodded, too scared to say anything.

Eager to please, I made a great show of dragging out the vacuum cleaner, hauling it into the front room.

My mother called out, 'Remember the corners. If you do, the middle takes care of itself. I don't want any of your slipshod efforts.'

An hour later, we dashed to school, and all day I immersed myself in lessons, refusing to think about the evening ahead. Far too soon the final bell rang. I hurried home, to scrub my face, hands and knees with Lifebuoy carbolic soap. Then, my reddened skin smelling of newly-washed laundry, I slipped on a clean red check school frock, white socks and polished red sandals.

'Come here.' My mother's voice was impatient as she kept checking the time by the cuckoo clock in the front room. She pulled a comb through my tangled hair and plaited it tightly, fastening the ends of the plaits with bright scarlet ribbons. My scalp tingled as she stood back, regarding her work with satisfaction.

Anxious to avoid the ordeal, Jill had already plaited her own hair, and we stood there, pictures of meek cleanliness. Our mother was smartly dressed in a black costume, the tailored jacket pinched in at the waist. Her curly hair was now tamed and her court shoes made her seem even taller than her five-foot-seven inches. She smiled as she looked down at her own costume.

'Right, we're ready. Now, remember all I've taught you.'

Behind the stage, waiting for my turn, I suddenly felt the ice of terror and turned round, to see Jill a few rows behind. Jill looked straight back. 'We have to win, we have to do what she wants,' she mouthed, and I relaxed. Of course we did; there was no option.

Then I was on stage, standing up straight, hands by my sides, gazing out at an imaginary spot on the back wall of the hall, aware of my mother sitting rigidly in the third row. The adjudicator caught my eye, and nodded. 'When you're ready, dear,' she said as she picked up her pen.

As I launched into the poem I was back in our front room, standing in the corner, with my mother instructing: 'You need a note of wonder in your voice when you come to ''oranges from Jaffa, and gold.'' Remember to lower your voice for ''misty English trees'' and, for goodness sake, don't forget the note of pride you need for ''and sights the hills of Devon…'' '

At ten- and- a- half and nine years, Jill and I were entirely biddable and frightened of defying our mother. We would not dream of protesting about the dreary hours of rehearsal, but I remembered my father, Dabber, sighing behind his paper and muttering, 'Violet, how much more of this reciting lark do we have to put up with?'

Then it was over, and I left the stage to wait for the results, and silently wished Jill good luck.

After the results for both our competition classes were announced, in relief, and for once with pleasure, we joined our mother in the audience. She beamed, flushed and happy. 'Well done.' Turning to the stranger beside her, she said, 'These are my daughters, and they've both won. I coached them myself.'

While the stranger murmured polite compliments, Jill and I exchanged embarrassed glances.

The poetry competition for younger children was next on the programme, and our mother decided to stay and listen. I sat by her, content. She was triumphant - the triumph was hers so the evening might be bearable. I gazed around me. The town hall was filling up rapidly, as competitors for later classes arrived. There was an expectant, nervous atmosphere. I looked up at the vaulted ceiling and felt proud that I had won in such a prestigious place. It was a moment of delight and I wriggled happily in my seat, prepared to enjoy seeing the little ones perform.

The competitors appeared on the stage, one by one. They were too young to be nervous, and each waited confidently for the adjudicator's signal to start.

Then a little girl of about six, whom I had never seen before, walked on to the stage, pretty and smiling. She was dressed as I was in a check cotton dress. Hers was blue. But unlike me, she had a natural poise and grace. I longed to have her Milly-Molly-Mandy haircut, a bob with a fringe. The girl's hair shone under the Town Hall lights, as she stood, happy and composed, looking out into the audience. Framed by the ornate stage curtains she had everyone's attention.

At a signal from the adjudicator she began to recite her poem. My mother's eyes were fixed on the girl. Suddenly she clutched her chest and gasped. The colour drained from her face which was now an unpleasant grey with red blotches. I felt alarmed and Jill, on the other side of her, whispered, 'Mum, are you feeling ill?'

The adjudicator retired to make her decisions, the hall broke out into chatter, and the people near us gave my mother curious glances.

'Shirley's here,' Jill said, and I heard the relief in her voice. 'She'll know what to do.' Our elder sister, Shirley, had come straight from work to join us, and when my mother saw her, she grabbed her arm and began to whisper urgently.

'Mum, how do you know?' Shirley's tone was reasonable. 'You can't possibly know.'

'I know, I know, of course I know. How could I not?' Tears began to run down her face; her body was shaking. 'She's mine. Look at our Judy, then look at her. They look like twins.' I looked over at the little girl. She was standing quietly with her teacher and some friends. Did I look like her? Was I as pretty as she was? I found that hard to believe.

'Mum, you need to go home.'

'The papers in the wardrobe...' she sobbed. 'They'll have her name on them.' She turned to me, eyes glittering and desperate. 'Judy, go over to that little girl with the short, dark bob and ask her what her name is.'

'Mum...'Shirley began again, but my mother pushed her aside. 'Judy, do as you're told, now.'

I looked from my mother to Shirley and back again. My mother shoved me and I made my way over to where the girl stood. I felt confused. Why had this girl upset Mum so much? How did Mum know her when Shirley, Jill and I did not? I jumped straight in. 'What's your name?'

The little girl's smile did not waver. 'Judy Woods.'

We stood looking at each other for a brief moment, two small children, one nine-years-old, the other just six, strangers with a shared name.

Chapter 2: 322 Luton Road

In November the year was dying. It was not a time for birth and regeneration, but my mother lay in labour for almost a week in that unforgiving month in 1943. The grey wartime misery echoed hers, and the weather was misty as though in sympathy. As she lay there, fighting her own battle to get her sixth baby to emerge into an uncertain world, the wireless reported that gales off France were making flying difficult for bombers.

Although I was Violet's sixth child, I was the first that was so reluctant to be born. My mother feared giving birth. When I was fourteen, she told me that each time she endured labour she hated all men with a deadly loathing. But with my birth, she said that she went through an experience so threatening, that the hatred gave way to a terrible fear that she would not survive.

My father, Aubrey, had cycled home from work for his mid-day meal. Afterwards he prepared to wheel his bicycle down the side passage, towards the front gate, for the mile ride uphill back to the iron foundry. Violet, agitated, appeared at the back door. 'Dabber, it's started.'

She always called him Dabber if in trouble.

Unless fuelled by political passion my father generally said little, so his response was terse: 'Don't leave it too long before you call for the midwife.' He swung his leg over the saddle and pedalled away.

Seven years earlier, in 1936, when her second baby, my sister Shirley, had been born, they had had a similar exchange. Then it had been a Wednesday lunchtime, up the hill on the other side of the road, in a different rented house, with an outside privy and a coal cellar. That time my father had added generously, 'You needn't bring up the coal; I'll do it when I come home.'

But the contractions had eased, and Violet had struggled down to the coal cellar to fill the scuttle, saying to Tony, the eldest, aged two, 'Stay at the top of the steps, wait for Mummy and be a good boy.'

Despite her exertions the contractions had paused, and she went to bed that night certain that her baby's birth was not, in fact, imminent. But, in the early hours, with the wind howling round the eaves and the snow piling higher, she had woken my father. 'Dabber, Dabber, it's coming after all. It won't be much longer, get the midwife now.'

After throwing on a few clothes, he had run out into the January gale, skidded and slid the bicycle over ground as crisp as biscuit, to the midwife's house. He couldn't rouse her by banging on the knocker, so he dug into the snow for a handful of gravel and threw it at the bedroom window. She opened it and shrugged off his urgency: 'The baby isn't due for another fortnight, it's just practising.'

My father got on his bike again, and slithered home to find my mother lying on the bedroom floor, distraught, beside the chamber pot where she had given birth, confusing the baby's arrival with the need to empty her bowels. The air was freezing, the panic tangible. Once more, he had dashed out into the harsh whiteness, banged on the door of the house next door, and begged the neighbour, Daisy Brown, to stay with his wife. Then he raced off to the doctor's house.

Young, newly qualified Dr Ashton came immediately, also on a bike, and found that the umbilical cord, still attached, had blinded baby Shirley in one eye. Gently he administered to mother and baby, and in fury, vowed aloud to get the midwife struck off.

Now, in wartime November, 1943, seven years later, enough time had passed for my mother to forget the terror she had felt. She had also given birth three more times in the intervening years, without any problem. However, by the time my father arrived home from the foundry he found her in distress and unable to cope.

Ten- year-old Tony and seven- year-old Shirley were doing their best to look after Roger aged five, Roy, three, and eighteen- month-old Jill. The new, local midwife was called, and cheerfully said nothing much was doing although the contractions were very strong. Plump and reassuring, she said that she would call again the next morning. 'But don't hesitate to call me if the baby decides to come in the night. Babies come when it's convenient for them, not us.'

The baby had still not arrived when the next morning dawned, grey and miserable. Day and night began to be one long painful blur for Violet. Her children could hear her whimpering when they woke in the dark, and in the daytime they fended for themselves, for their father had to work. As foundry foreman, Aubrey Darby could not be spared from the important war munitions manufacture at Bagshawe Conveyors, where he supervised the manufacture of conveyor belts for Royal Ordnance factories, and caterpillar tracks for Bren gun carriers. And as a father of a large family he dare not cut his income. Kindly neighbours brought dishes, ill-spared in a time of rationing. They remembered the eggs given so freely by my mother from our chickens in the back garden, when my less generous father was at work. Most eggs had to be handed in to the authorities for distribution, but most people ignored that dictate.

Upstairs in the front room my mother lay in the bed behind the door. Opposite were utility wardrobes, bought proudly when they had moved to the house six years previously. She lay, twisting the pink satin eiderdown between her fingers, the veins on her rough, house worked hands raised in tension and pain. The windows were low and deep, and from her bed she could see Dunstable Downs, partly shrouded in mist, grey-green at that time of the year, and tinged with frost as the sun rose on her suffering each morning. Bluebell Woods, where her children explored happily in the Spring, bringing back tangled bunches of delicate, musky smelling blooms, lurked darkly towards the back of the downs. A woman of vivid imagination, she wondered whether the world outside would ever be hers again.

She ate nothing. Sips of water were all she could endure. She coughed frequently as the needles of pain shot through her lungs. And throughout those terrifying days and nights the rhythmic contractions cruelly tortured. When necessary she struggled from her bed to sit on the chamber pot to pass dark, evil smelling urine, which Shirley would carry downstairs, to empty in the lavatory outside the back door.

Downstairs the children were unnaturally quiet. There were no squabbles, no noise, merely an exchange of anxious glances and tremendous relief every time normality was restored by an adult knocking on the door with food or a cheerful word. Tony and Roger were sent to school, where a hot mid-day meal was served, while Shirley cared for Roy and Jill.

As the week wore on, even the blasé midwife began to express concern. She had stopped fielding my father's anxious enquiries with cheerful platitudes. My mother's condition was deteriorating fast. By Sunday morning she was having trouble breathing. My father ignored the midwife and sent for Dr Ashton who was shocked by what he saw. 'Why wasn't I called earlier?' he asked the midwife, 'Couldn't you see she has double pneumonia?

'I thought that Mrs. Darby would be all right once the baby arrived.' The midwife sounded hesitant.

'I would rather you had not conjectured, but called someone who had greater knowledge.' The doctor's tone was savage. 'Then he turned to my father. 'We're going to have to deliver the baby as soon as possible; the pneumonia has been brought on by days spent lying in labour...hard labour.'

At seven o'clock that Sunday evening the doctor delivered a screaming baby girl. 'Keep the baby away from her mother,' he ordered the midwife, 'we mustn't risk infecting the child. God knows what damage has been done already.' His tone softened as he spoke to my father: 'You're going to have to find someone to look after the baby. Your wife needs to be taken to hospital immediately.'

Outside, in the dark street, neighbours watched in sympathetic silence as my mother was carried to the ambulance. She beckoned a tearful, stricken Shirley to her side and whispered, 'You can name the baby.' Then the ambulance doors were slammed shut.

Over the next few weeks as my mother lay in hospital, my father faced the problem of the care of his children. He had to work and he had to find medical fees. This was five years before Bevan introduced the National Health Service and health did not come cheaply.

The immediate problem was what to do about the new baby. Then, one of the neighbours, Mrs. Tottle, knocked on the door.

'I hear you need someone to look after the little one,' she said. 'I could do that. I'm used to babies. I don't charge much.'

My father knew the scruffy, friendly woman vaguely by sight, and that she lived round the corner in Evelyn Road. He knew that her son, Johnny, played with his third child, my brother, Roger. There was no choice. He turned to Mrs. Tottle. 'Thank you,' he said, 'I should be very grateful for your help.'

A brief discussion followed. Shirley found all the outgrown baby clothes she could, and hastily parcelled the threadbare nappies, already used by five Darby children. A very small sum of money was agreed: Mrs. Tottle was grateful for anything to eke out her tight budget.

Mrs. Tottle took me home. I was barely two hours old, but she swaddled me tightly against the chill and thickening mist.

'Get on your bike and ride to your grandmother's,' my father said to Tony. 'Tell her what has happened and ask her to come over first thing in the morning.'

Tony wrapped his navy gabardine mac round him, and pushed his bike down the side passage. He peered through the now dense fog and set off for Grandma West's house in Limbury, three miles away. Very early the next morning she arrived at 322, calm and reliable. She knew that she couldn't manage to look after all the children. She took Shirley, Roy and Jill back to her house and left Tony and Roger in our home with my father. Shirley went home with Grandma to help look after Roy and Jill. And every day the seven-year-old would make her way back home on the bus to collect the washing, and replace it with clean clothes washed by hand in Grandma's deep, cracked sink. Shirley helped Grandma wring out the clothes and dry them on the wooden clothes horse round the fire. Then Shirley heated the iron on the stove, and Grandma urged her not to burn herself.

Within a few days Jill had been sent to Chesham to Grandma's other daughter, Lily, and her husband Ted.

In the meantime Tony biked to the hospital each morning, to collect the milk the nurses had expressed from my mother. Mrs. Tottle fed it to me over the twenty-four hours.

Each night Aubrey made his way to the Luton and Dunstable Hospital for the meagre half hour allowed for visiting, retracing the bicycle ride Tony made in the morning. And each night, as he entered that overpoweringly antiseptic world, with the reek of disinfectant clinging to his nostrils, my father would receive the news that his wife was failing.

One evening a consultant was waiting to see him, but Aubrey insisted on seeing Violet first. He was horrified by what he saw, a circle of branded, festering skin on each breast. The pitiful sight of this wasted woman, gasping for breath filled him with distress, swiftly followed by fury.

He strode out into the corridor where the doctor waited, one hand raised. 'I can explain. A nurse in a hurry forgot to cool the breast pump when she took it out of the steriliser. I am very sorry. But we have more pressing concerns than your wife's burns, I'm afraid. She seems to be sinking fast.'

My father used anger to mask other, deeper emotions. He stood in the green and cream painted corridor, in despair. 'For God's sake stop expressing milk from her. I'm no doctor but even I can work out that you are draining the few resources she has left to fight with. The energy she is expending making that milk for the baby, is killing her.'

'You might be right,' the doctor conceded. 'But stopping the milk isn't going to save her. Mr. Darby, you are going to have to face the fact that your wife is a very sick woman.'

'I faced that fact from day one,' said my father, fighting back his anger. 'And it wasn't me who burnt her. I'm telling you now that no more milk is to be sucked from her.'

His voice faltered, his bravado fading. His six children were being cared for in four different homes, his wife lay dying a few yards away, he was working in the white heat and grime of a foundry twelve hours a day. He held out his hands. 'Is there anything you can do?'

'There is.' The doctor was careful in his response. 'You've heard of M and B?'

My father nodded. 'They gave that drug to Churchill earlier this year. He hailed it as a wonder drug. Certainly cured *his* pneumonia.'

The doctor permitted himself a wry smile. 'Yes, but he thought it better not to reveal that it's a German discovery. Not until this war is over anyway.'

My father smiled in return and the tension relaxed between the two men.

'Anyway, I think we should try it on Mrs. Darby.' The doctor's tone was brisk. 'Immediately.'

The next evening the doctor was waiting again, smiling cautiously. 'It's early days, Mr. Darby, but the improvement over the last few hours has been excellent.

Now there is every chance she will make a complete recovery... And by the way, we've stopped the milk.'

It was several weeks before my mother returned home. She was frail and thin, her movements hesitant, her eyes showing the suffering she had endured.

Jill did not want to come home from Chesham. She had spent long enough there with Auntie Lily and Uncle Ted to assume the kindly couple were her parents. When she realised that they were going to leave her at Luton Road, she was inconsolable.

Auntie Lily looked nervously at Uncle Ted and cleared her throat. 'We'd like to keep Jill,' she said to her sister. 'She and our Jennifer have got on so well. There's very little difference in their age. We'd give her a good home, you can be certain of that.'

My mother tightened her lips and frowned. 'It's very kind of you, but she's my daughter not yours.'

Auntie Lily did not heed the warning signs. 'But she's been so happy with us, Violet. She was so jumpy when she first came to us,' adding hastily, 'I expect it was because she was missing you. But she's rosy now, and smiles all the time.'

'Stop it. Jill is mine.' My mother began to sob. 'Dabber, don't let them suggest such things. *My* mother had to give away her little girl; I'm not losing mine.'

Lily said quietly, 'It didn't do me any harm, Violet. I'm only thinking of you and how much you've got to cope with.'

My father looked at my mother and intervened. 'No one is going to split this family. Lily, we do appreciate all you have done for Jill but she stays here. This is her home, and we are her family.'

Auntie Lily said goodbye to Jill, and the little girl clung to her, screaming, 'Don't leave me here, don't leave me Mummy.' She refused to be comforted by her real mother, and it was Shirley who finally calmed her, and held her until she fell asleep in exhaustion.

My mother, weak and tearful, said, 'Where's my other baby? Why isn't she here?'

'I thought it would be too much for you today,' said my father. 'I've asked Mrs. Tottle to keep her for a little longer.'

'I want her now. Are you trying to turn her against me too?'

My father sighed. 'Tony, go round the corner and ask Mrs. Tottle for the baby. Be careful how you carry her.' Tony disappeared and returned five minutes later clutching a bundle of white shawl. He handed the bundle to my mother.

Shakily, my mother held out her arms. Suddenly she shrieked. 'She's covered in a rash, and looks thin and sore! What have they done to her? My babies don't look like this! Take it away!'

'Violet,' said my father, his tone reasonable, 'babies do get rashes. And she didn't have the best of starts in life. Give her to me; you've frightened her with your crying.'

I was taken back to Mrs. Tottle for another few weeks until Violet could at least look after herself. My father set up a bed in our front room and she lay there overseeing the household.

Grandma West came over on the bus to help as much as she could, and always took home the dirty washing. Tony and Shirley helped with chores, cooking, and care of the younger children. Shirley had been helping since she was five when she had stood on a stool at the kitchen sink to do the washing up.

Slowly my mother's health returned. I was brought home to stay, and normality seemed to return to the household. And as she grew stronger, and was able to care for the family again, my mother became bored with her daily routine of cooking and cleaning. One day she slipped down to the corner shop, fifty yards away, leaving Jill and me asleep upstairs. She became engrossed in conversation and it was an hour before she returned home.

Meanwhile, Grandma West had stepped off the bus from Leagrave and walked through the unlocked back door. Hearing a crying baby, she went upstairs and found Jill and me in the cot together, both hungry, and lying in sodden sheets.

My mother returned to find a shocked Grandma busy drying the sheets.

'You didn't tell me you were coming.' Violet's tone was accusing.

Grandma narrowed her lips. 'That much is clear. How could you go out and leave these babies alone? Look at the state of them. And the bedding...Violet, there are maggots in the bedding.'

'I had to go to the shop if there was to be anything for their tea tonight. What right have you to come here, uninvited, unannounced, and attack me? You have no idea how hard it is for me, looking after six children.'

Grandma looked at her daughter in sadly. 'I know it's hard work, Violet. And I know what a woeful time you've had. But these are babies who need you to look after them properly. I help you all I can, but mostly you don't want me here.'

Neither had noticed Shirley's arrival home from school. She stood there anxiously, looking from face to face. Grandma saw her first. 'No more discussion. It will only upset the children.'

My mother erupted in loud, furious tears. 'How dare you come here and tell me what to do, and say that I don't look after my children properly. You are an interfering, old cow. Get out and stay out.'

Grandma quietly gathered her belongings together and left while Mum alternately pleaded and demanded that Shirley should say what a good mother she was. 'And you tell that old cow how good I am when you next see her - you can also tell her she's never coming here again.'

When my father came home, the outburst was renewed, as he received a highly dramatised version of Grandma's words. He liked his mother-in-law, and treated her with great respect. He was uncomfortable with what he heard. 'Perhaps you took it the wrong way. I'm sure she meant no harm.'

'No harm,' screamed my mother, 'no harm. You weren't here, so how the hell do you know?'

My father sighed, and picked up the newspaper, his usual refuge.

Grandma did not return until several weeks later, at her son-in-law's urging. Then she took care with what she said, for fear that her daughter would see it as criticism and throw her out again.

As Violet's health improved her temper blazed. Rows echoed round the house. My father's anxiety over money was giving him sleepless nights and making him ill, though still he struggled on. Every day he coughed and wheezed his way up the hill on his bike.

Each night the arguments started. The atmosphere was like a tinder-box. Tony and Shirley waited in dread for the bitter words, as they hid in the corner of the room, trying to make themselves invisible. Upstairs, the younger children would hear raised voices, and turn restlessly.

Firstly there were the bills for my mother's medical care, in those pre- National Health Service days. Then there was her belief that money could always be found from somewhere. As her strength improved so did her desire to spend.

My father said that there was no money.

'What about the money you earned lecturing to the police at the beginning of the war?'

It was true that he had earned some extra money when he attended a course on the recognition and dismantling of bombs, and had come out with a score of one hundred per cent. Then he had been offered the lucrative evening sessions, passing on his knowledge to the local police.

'You spent most of that money. You couldn't wait to get your hands on it. The rest went on hospital fees, and we still owe the final payment on those.'

'What about the money won from the National Savings slogan competition?' she wanted to know. Again, it was true that my father had won some money when he had coined the slogan, *Save until it hurts and give the pain to Hitler.* This winning entry had been strung in a huge banner across the town hall.

My father's laugh had nothing to do with humour. 'How far do you think that prize-money went? We've got no bloody money.'

Things slowly got worse. And even my mother began to realise the gravity of the situation. Before she had had her children she had always enjoyed her job, in the office at Electrolux, a domestic appliance factory. Ironically she had been a book keeper. When the children were born she had given up the job, and now she missed the company and shared laughter. A new state day nursery had opened half a mile away, and took children as young as six months. She suggested that Jill and I should be registered there. There was a fee but it was also subsidised to persuade women into work. Roy was due to start school in September, joining Roger and Shirley at Evelyn Road, the primary school round the corner, and Tony had won a scholarship a year early to Dunstable Grammar School and was already a pupil there.

My father was delighted as this would mean my mother could return to work. Tony would turn eleven that September and Shirley would be eight and a half. Both parents considered these two children sufficiently old and responsible to look after the others before and after school. My mother promised to start applying for jobs. In the meantime, final demands were pouring through the door. As my father was treasurer of the firm's Christmas Club, and collected money from his colleagues each week, my mother couldn't see why he should not borrow some of it to pay off the outstanding bills. After all, she would be working very soon, and so it could be paid back in good time.

At first my father was scandalised. He protested that he was in a position of trust; it was immoral and criminal. But as she continued to apply pressure, and threatening letters arrived, he gave way, and reluctantly paid bills with the Christmas Club money, also handing over more to buy the clothes she insisted she needed for a new job.

As September turned into October and the mellow evenings became crisper and colder, My father became increasingly anxious about how to repay the money. The employees were due to receive their savings at the end of the second week in December. My father noticed that my mother was not applying for jobs. He asked her why, at first tentatively, then with mounting agitation. She replied that she was still convalescent, that she had enough to do looking after six children, that she would think about it, that she would get a job when she was ready. This became a familiar pattern. She played her game with consummate skill, and my father's anxiety gave way to alarm and anger. 'You said that if I borrowed that money you would get a job to pay it back. For God's sake, Violet, if that money isn't returned in good time, before anyone finds out, I'll be sentenced to hard labour.'

The children listened in silence and terror. Only Tony and Shirley really understood. As adults, when recounting the events of that time, they were still shaken at the memory of my mother's desire to hurt, and my father's despair. She was bored with her daily routine and the struggle to run the household on what my father could afford to give her, she was still weak from her illness, and the only way she seemed to be able to express her feelings was by goading her husband.

The tangibly bad atmosphere affected the whole family. Quarrels broke out freely between the children as they lashed out aimlessly at each other. As the October nights lengthened, the house slowly suffocated under the tension. Roy settled into school, Jill and I became used to the nursery, benefiting from its order and structure, receiving both breakfast and lunch. None of us wanted to be at home where we were forced to listen to the battle of wills between our parents.

One evening my father came home from work, beaten. He was staring at a prison sentence, and with it the inevitable disintegration of his family. As he slumped into his armchair my mother said casually, 'I start work on Monday.'

Not only did she start work in an accounts office, but her salary was nearly as much as my father's. The money was paid back into the Christmas Club Fund just in time, and Shirley and Tony remembered that Christmas in 1944 as being the best ever. Toys were bought, food and drink was plentiful, and an atmosphere of happiness replaced the tension and misery of the preceding months. It was the beginning of the good times.

My mother was always gregarious, and now she had the money to spend evenings in the company of like-minded, affluent people. These friends were mostly men, or couples wealthy enough to employ help with their children; certainly they would have baby sitters. In the Darby household, Tony, eleven, and Shirley, nine, looked after younger siblings ranging from one to seven years.

One of my parents' friends was a history teacher from Tony's grammar school, who worshipped my mother all her adult life, another, a master builder with a thriving business, and then there were the Prouds. Arnold Proud had a high position at Bagshawe Conveyors, where my father worked, and Trudie Proud, admired by my mother, was gently spoken and beautifully groomed. She would not have dreamed of going out to work. Finally, there was Mildred Stott, a wealthy American friend, who had known my mother from schooldays. These friends would gather in the lounge bars of up-market pubs, drinking, chatting and laughing. My mother revelled in these evenings, which perhaps enabled her to forget her drudgery and responsibilities, but my father would have preferred spending the evenings quietly listening to the wireless or reading. But he gave way to her demands and dragged himself out with her most nights. Always the centre of attention, she seemed as if she was frenetically making up for the time she had spent close to death. Driven by nervous energy, however, she frequently paid for her lifestyle with crippling headaches and vomiting.

Each work day my mother would leave the house by 8 am. Shirley dressed Jill and me ready for the nursery, and Tony prepared breakfast for Roger and Roy. This was bread and dripping, or on rare occasions when there was enough milk, cereal. Then Tony would get out his handmade cart, a strengthened orange box on wheels, and fix it to the back of his bike with an old washing line. Jill and I would be lifted into the cart and he would set off up the hill. We bumped helplessly up and down all the way. The neighbours were shocked at this highly dangerous mode of transport for a toddler and baby, and complained to my father. Tony hid his cart and brought it out again the next morning when my father had gone to work. Without this transport, he would have been forced to wheel us to the nursery in the battered pram. This would have made him late for school, and subject to punishment.

Back home Shirley put the communal, smelly flannel round Roger and Roy's faces, before sending them off round the corner to school. Then she did the washing up before running off after them, reaching the school gates as the whistle blew.

After school, Tony collected Jill and me from the nursery, put us in the orange box, and took us back to the house in Luton Road. He would find Shirley slicing chunks of bread, before smothering them with margarine and jam. Between them they sat Roger, Roy and Jill round the table, while I was put in the high chair. Washed down with milky tea, the bread and jam had to be enough for an evening meal. There was nothing else. Even I managed the rough hewn bread, cut into small pieces.

Once again the family flannel would be wrung out in a bowl of warm water, and Lifebuoy carbolic soap massaged on to the cloth. This was rubbed round four faces and hands, and the kitchen towel, grimy and damp, was then applied to our infant skins.

Jill and Judy at the nursery Christmas party 1946
Jill aged 4 (extreme right) Judy aged 3 (next to Jill)

322 Luton Road was an average sized semi- detached house. At that time we rented it from a private landlord, although later my father would obtain a mortgage and buy it. It was not sufficient for a large growing family, especially as we lived in the back room during the winter months to save fuel. Most families at the time would adopt the same strategy, but it meant if we were all there together, most of the children would have to sit on the floor, fighting with our collie dog, Lassie, to be near the fire. There was also a table as the kitchen was too small to

contain one, dining chairs, a settee and two armchairs. In the alcove by the fire was a bookcase, and I think all the children read every one of the eclectic mix, from the set of encyclopaedia, whose headings I can still quote by heart - A to BAD, BAD to BRI, BRI to CHR, CHR to DEN…- to *The Diary of A Nobody* and *The Ragged Trousered Philanthropist*. When my father died I took the bookcase home; no one else in the family wanted it. My husband, a teacher of physics, wood and metalwork, and a gifted carpenter, eyed it critically, but made no comment as he fixed its uneven sides. I kept that bookcase for years, long after it should have gone to a tip, and felt sharp guilt when I finally let it go.

On the floor was a patterned carpet flanked by polished floorboards. Sitting on the floor in front of the fire, six year-old Jill taught me to tie my shoe laces when I was five.

In the early years of the war my father kept a chart of battle progress on the wall in the back room, and when he came home from work, would throw the children into the hall while he listened to the news.

The lavatory was in the back garden, and the bathroom upstairs, which held a bath and washbasin, was rarely used. Baths were infrequent, and the whole family used the same water. Because of the ingrained grime from the foundry my father bathed last, my mother first, and the children in order of age. By the time my father gingerly stepped into the tepid water, it was filthy.

There were three bedrooms. My parents had the front bedroom with its view of the downs. The other two had a double bed in each, and the boys slept in one, and the girls in the other. Light bulbs were always scarce in all our homes. This was simple bad management, for as each bulb perished it was never replaced. Yet my mother was scared of the dark so the landing light was always on, and if it failed a substitute from another room was found, leaving that room bereft of light. There were no lights in the children's rooms at Luton Road. Tony and Shirley put us to bed every night before our parents came home from work, and then the bedroom doors were firmly shut. Downstairs Shirley and Tony prepared a meal. My father arrived home and expected a cup of tea to be waiting for him, ungratefully labelling it 'piss' as it was handed over. Sometimes he would refer to it as the 'piss which passeth all understanding' thinking that was amusing. He would be very tired while my fragile mother would come home full of life and anecdotes from her day, looking forward to going out for the evening.

Violet's favourite drink was gin. Usually it made her happy and light- hearted. But at times it made her cruel, although she would have termed it witty. She drank socially, and always outside the home because alcohol was only kept in our house at Christmas. Sometimes, when she came home after a night out, she would call up the stairs to wake Shirley, and tell her to come downstairs.

'Where did I get you from?' Her eyes would sparkle with malice.

'You're bandy-legged and cross-eyed.' Then came a little tinkling laugh. 'You only need to start talking with your father's common accent, and you'll be a complete mess. Go on, back to bed, then I won't have to look at you.'

On one occasion a quarrel broke out between my parents as they neared home, and she rushed ahead into the house.

'Shirley, Shirley, where are you?'

The urgent tone brought Shirley stumbling downstairs from her bed.

She sat on the third stair from the bottom, and through the banister rails, watched her mother go into the kitchen. Wild eyed, and very drunk, she called out, 'Shirley, you are to be a good girl and look after your brothers and sisters. I won't be here.' Then she turned on the gas oven and kneeling down, put her head in it.

Terrified, Shirley ran to the front door, and bumped into Aubrey coming in.

'Dad, Dad, save Mum, please. She's going to die. Please save her, Dad.'

'Violet, what the fucking hell are you playing at?' Switching the oven off with one hand, my father grasped a clump of her hair with the other, and hauled her to her feet. Then he thumped her as hard as he could, blacking her eye, and bruising the whole of one side of her face. Eyes blazing, he put his face close to hers and hissed, 'Don't you dare frighten those children again. You cruel, fucking cow. Play your sordid little games with me, if you must, but leave them alone.'

Shirley crept upstairs to bed, breath held, trying desperately not to make a sound. She knew exactly what would happen. The next morning, as soon as her father had left for work, fury was unleashed. 'If you hadn't pretended to be scared, I wouldn't have got bashed. It's all your fault that my poor eye and face are like this. Look.' She leaned closer to Shirley, and the child could smell her rancid, gin-sour breath. 'I can't go to work today and let anyone see me like this. How dare you come between me and your father.' The blow sent Shirley stumbling across the room, and she got to her feet clutching her bleeding face and rapidly colouring eye.

'Let's see how you like going to school with a black eye,' said her mother with satisfaction. 'And remember to tell them that you have been fighting with your brother.'

That evening my father came home with some steak. Putting his arms round my mother, he kissed her and she began to sniffle. Then he unwrapped his parcel with great care, and helped her sit down. He applied the steak to her black eye, and she cried out in theatrical pain. Later he cooked it for their evening meal, and they chatted and laughed as if nothing had happened.

Sometime during the course of the evening my father noticed Shirley's bruised face. 'How did you get that?'

My mother intervened swiftly. 'Tony hit her because she took his pen.'

Aubrey compressed his lips and looked at his two oldest children with anger. 'How many times have I told you children not to fight?'

Tony had been absorbed in his homework, sitting at the table, brow furrowed, but he looked up startled. 'No one has taken my pen. And I haven't hit anyone.'

My father's eyes darkened, 'Any more lies and you go to bed.'

'But…'

'Get to bloody bed, right now.'

'I haven't finished my homework.'

As his father advanced across the room, hand raised, Tony slammed his books together, and ran out of the room, shutting the door as loudly as he dared.

Chapter 3: My Grandparents

My mother was wild, hysterical and dangerous at times. But so was Alfred, her father, the grandfather I never knew.

Alfred was a sewing machine salesman and spent much of his time on the road, selling machines to housewives and small companies, virtual sweatshops. One of his duties was to collect weekly payments from the women who either rented their machines, or were buying them on hire purchase, 'on tick' or 'the glad and sorry' - glad to have the item, sorry that it needed payment.

Alfred was the ideal salesman. Tall, handsome, courteous and friendly, with dark hair and a ready smile. He was also a Lothario. It was during his travels that he met the inexperienced, trusting Maudie Fisher, my grandmother, a tiny, delicately built girl, with a mop of curly hair which she brushed back severely. She was working at one of the big houses he visited. When he met and courted unworldly Maudie, she fell in love at once. He was twenty-seven when they married, while she was two years younger. Her naivety allowed Alfred to seduce her, so that by the time they married, Maudie was pregnant.

Maudie might have dreamed of a long and happy marriage, but she was destined to be a widow before she was forty, and to watch her husband die in excruciating pain.

It is likely that Alfred caught syphilis sometime before he married my grandmother. Statistics show that the most probable time for a man to become infected is between the ages of twenty and twenty-nine, when he is at his most sexually active. The first symptom of this terrible disease, a chancre or sore on the genitals, rectum or mouth, lasts a few weeks before healing spontaneously. Usually, no ill-effects are felt, so there is a good chance that the sore might be overlooked. The contagious period is over within a few months, although it is possible to become re-infected, then it enters a dormant phase which might last several years before destroying every organ in the body, including the brain.

At the time of her marriage in 1905, my grandmother knew nothing of Alfred's condition, nor would she have been aware that such a condition existed. It is unlikely that Alfred knew he had syphilis, or that an early agonising death awaited him. He had certainly ignored the transitory symptoms, not realising their significance. But as any cure for the disease was still largely controversial and experimental, recognition of his condition might not have helped him.

Within three years of marriage Maudie had given birth to two sons. The eldest, my Uncle Jim, was healthy but Tich, the second son, was sickly, and he died from kidney failure at the age of forty-four. My mother, Violet, was physically ill and vulnerable to emotional instability for much of her adult life. She died at the age of forty-nine from a variety of complaints, including cerebral haemorrhage, pyelonephritis and hypertension. Her sight was failing, her constant thirst indicated diabetes, and her behaviour was increasingly irrational. Although syphilis is not hereditary, it is contagious, and there is no way of knowing whether Grandfather West had infected my grandmother. Although she lived until she was seventy-seven that does not mean that she had not contracted syphilis, as in some cases it can cure itself spontaneously. On the evidence it is possible, even probable, that syphilis might well have placed a part in the premature deaths of two of Alfred's children.

In 1911 it became clear that Alfred was suffering from some puzzling complaint. Grandma became alarmed at his symptoms. She always kept her silence and her children were never told the reason for Grandfather's gradual loss of control over both temper and body. Alfred's muscles began to weaken as locomotor ataxia, or syphilis of the spinal cord, set in. He found it difficult to walk, staggering round in pain, with an unco-ordinated lumbering gait. But it is doubtful that his illness was diagnosed at that stage. Although syphilis was far more prevalent than today, little was understood about its progression. It is often termed 'the great imitator' as many of its symptoms are indistinguishable from other diseases.

Alfred went on to father two daughters, my mother Violet, and Lily, before he became too weak to stir from bed. He lay there, helpless and incontinent, and then the disease moved inexorably to attack his brain, causing irrational rage and confusion.

My mother was born in 1912, and she remembers being terrified of his ugly moods as his pain became more intense. Around that time the doctor became aware of the nature of his illness, for his death certificate states that locomotor ataxia had been present for six years. The length of time he had suffered from the earlier stages of syphilis was open to conjecture, for the doctor who certified death, had also written 'specific disease' with a large question mark next to 'years'. The shock for my gentle grandmother must have been tremendous, but she rallied in her quiet, determined way and nursed Alfred to the end.

And the end was bitter. The pain intensified yet further as his death grew nearer. His body became totally ulcerated and his limbs lost all power. My grandmother did not reveal the true nature of his illness to her children, then or ever. The shame was too great and also she may have feared having the disease.

Finally Alfred died. His torture over, his body was placed in a coffin in the parlour, to lie there until his funeral a week later.

With Alfred's death in 1917, Maudie faced serious problems. Her youngest daughter, Lily, was less than three years old, and Maudie needed to work. So Lily was farmed out to her brother-in-law and his wife, in Chesham. Lily was never to come home again to live permanently, but each week Grandma made the long bus journey from Leagrave to Chesham, some twenty miles. Grandma must have taken comfort from the fact that Lily was happy, for it had broken her heart to part with her young daughter. But she was a stoical woman, who accepted the inevitable. She had no chance of working and looking after Lily. The other children could go to school, and if they missed their little sister at first, they were young, and other matters quickly occupied their minds. And Maudie was much too sensitive and generous a mother to allow them to see her distress.

Grandma Maudie West 1925 aged 45

As Grandma had refused to break contact with her daughter, she was never to experience the shock my mother received when seeing her daughter for the first time six years after her birth. Her decision must have been coloured by the fact that Lily was happy in her new home, and the young, self-absorbed Violet would not have noticed her mother's sorrow. However, my mother never told Grandma about the adoption of her seventh child and made numerous excuses not to see her during the months when the pregnancy was evident.

As she grew up Violet was indulged. She was the only girl at home, spoilt by mother and brothers. A photograph of her, taken at the age of fourteen, suggests an air of quiet confidence, as if she is aware of her looks, knowing she is admired. Her hair is fashionably bobbed to below her ears, a dark, shining cap with a natural wave. She is unsmiling, her lips firm. The jaw is strong, giving a hint of her wilful personality. But her eyes are dark and vulnerable, underlining the complexity of her nature.

Violet rarely considered the consequences of her actions, for she quickly learned that there were usually none. As a small child I would listen in awe when she told me that. Grandma would remonstrate, 'Oh Violet, how could you!' but her tone was always too gentle to excite fear of repercussion. Her eldest brother, Jim, tried to take on parental authority but she was much too bright and devious to succumb to that. She told me when I was thirteen, that her mother and Jim forbade her to bleach her beautiful dark, curly hair when she was the same age. She listened to them gravely, then went out into their tiny scullery and dyed her hair to a brassy blonde. I held my breath. 'Did you get into terrible trouble?'

My mother laughed. 'Of course not.'

Ironically, she would have beaten her own children black and blue for such defiance, followed by another good hiding when my father came home.

Violet 1930 - aged 18

In 1926, when she was fourteen, Violet left school. She began work in an office, showing skill in book-keeping. This brought her promotion with an even greater sense of her own importance. But what mattered most to her, was that she had money to spend as she wished. Life began to be exciting. She enjoyed and was flattered by the attention from the men she worked with. Away from her mother's scrutiny she could laugh and flirt without her irritating, if gentle, reproaches.

It was then she met Aubrey Darby.

A few miles away Aubrey had grown up with *his* mother. At the age of twenty-one he still lived with her. He also had been raised as the youngest child of a mother struggling to cope without her husband's income.

Mary Ann Darby appears to be a contradictory character, a careful, responsible mother, who wanted only that her children should be able to raise themselves out of poverty. In this sense she and Maudie West had much in common. In very different ways both were abandoned by their husbands. Alfred West died from syphilis: the philandering Walter Darby deserved the same.

In other ways the two women were very different. Mary Ann had her own fluid interpretation of veracity: she had no qualms about lying about her age on official documents such as marriage certificates, and so the dates and ages on birth and death certificates, and censuses, don't tally.

Like Maudie, Mary Ann went into service when she was twelve, and nearly eight years later met and married Herbert Goddard. He was only sixteen. On the marriage certificate Mary Ann's age is recorded as sixteen, Herbert's nineteen. Perhaps Mary Ann did not want it to be known she was older than her husband, although as the ages for the couple are reversed, it is possible that it was a clerical error. If so, it was one that Mary Ann did not wish to correct. What also makes such a mistake unlikely, is that she took six years off her age when she married Walter Darby, thirteen years later. He was also younger than Mary Ann, by six years. Yet the 1911 Census records her as two years older than Walter. It is hardly surprising that her children were always confused about how old she was.

In 1895, after thirteen years of marriage, Herbert Goddard died of tuberculosis. He was thirty. For most of those years Mary Ann would have nursed an increasingly sick husband. There were four children to consider, one boy, and three girls, including twins. There was also a lodger, taken in to supplement the meagre family income. This lodger, a cousin of Herbert's, was Walter Darby, my grandfather.

Herbert died at the end of January, and by early April, Mary Ann had married Walter. This might well have been a shrewd move to save her from the workhouse, but the fact that she was pregnant with Walter's baby, does give the matter a different conclusion. This was backstreet living, where survival was key, and little time was given to considerations of sexual morality.

Walter was only five foot six and weighed barely nine stone. Part of the reason for this might well have been malnutrition. This delicate physique was inherited by only one of his children, my father.

Walter Darby - Boer War and First World War Soldier

Walter fought in the Boer War, and at its conclusion he left the army. He became a general labourer, turning his hand to whatever work he could get. This, together with his annuity from the Boer War, gave the family an adequate living, and the Darby's were considered well off by the standards of the time. Walter managed to change that, by wasting money on extra-marital relationships.

Walter frequently left home, only to return when his latest affair was over. My father records in his book, *A View from the Alley*:

No star pinpointed the location of my birth, yet my father who was drunk at the time, said it was 'a bloody miracle'

My father had thought that Mary Ann was forty-nine at the time of his birth, but she was forty-three. He writes:

The old midwife, without conceding an immaculate conception, warned I would either be an imbecile or commit murder.

When Aubrey was six, Walter stopped returning home, but set up house with a woman, round the corner. My father remembered being dressed in his oldest clothes and sent round to the house where his father was lodging, to ask for money. His mother's humiliation stayed in his memory.

Finally Walter left the area for good, and the family had no idea where he had gone. But records show he went to Nottingham where it seems he made a bigamous marriage.

Nothing more is known of Walter until the early 1940s, when one day Walter turned up at 322 Luton Road. It was a weekday afternoon and my father was at work. Walter, shabby and seedy looking, tried to muster his old patter: 'You are a beautiful woman; my son is a lucky man.'

When my father came home, he got no further than the hall. 'Dabber, your father is here. I've put him in the front room with a cup of tea.'

'You've done what!' This was no question, but an explosion of sheer fury. My father seized Walter's collar, the tea cup falling into the hearth and smashing irrecoverably.

No conversation. No comment. Walter was literally dragged down the hall and kicked out the front door.

My mother stood uncomprehendingly in the hall. 'He seemed such a nice old man. I thought you'd be pleased to see your father. You told me he was dead.'

My father said nothing. He straightened the runner in the hall and fetched a broom and piece of card, to clear up the broken remains of the cup. An unusual quiet hung over the house that evening, but not another word was uttered on the subject.

Desperation had driven Walter to seek out his son. He was in his seventies, living in destitution in Nottingham. It was there he died, in 1948, in a hostel for down-and-outs. He fell and fractured his hip, and the shock proved too much for the old man. The coroner provided the information for the death certificate so it is probable that none of Walter's family knew what had happened to him, or even where he was.

Mary Ann Darby 1922 - aged 50

Back in Luton, Mary Ann had struggled to raise her family. My father may have said 'her word was law', but while she worked long hours he felt free to roam the streets with his pals. He found a job with Mr. Clarke the butcher, and worked there, before and after school. When Aubrey developed appendicitis, it was kind Mr. Clarke who diagnosed what was wrong, after Gran, the local self-styled midwife and layer-out of bodies, had prescribed castor oil, and the doctor had charged half a crown to declare it was jaundice. My father wrote of Mr. Clarke:

His knowledge of sick animals stood me in good stead, for he asked Ma to get more expert advice and he would foot the bill.

My father was taken to hospital for his appendix removal; but as it had already burst he spent several weeks there. In a pre-anti-biotic age he was lucky to survive.

Aubrey was happy in hospital and didn't want to leave:

I dreaded the reality outside those walls.

His mother bought him a new outfit to wear for the journey home on the tram, *short nicks, Norfolk jacket and cap with ear flaps.* The conductor commented that Aubrey looked pale.

She countered by asking him if he expected to see a Red Indian. I relaxed, contented. Ma was still the same.

When he was twelve, my father took the Labour examination, which allowed boys who reached the required standard to leave school, and start full –time work. Mary Ann was against this, but Aubrey was adamant, for he felt that he had learned all that the sparse curriculum was offering. He passed, and the Headteacher wrote in his log book that it was 'very discouraging,' to see such intelligent boys leaving. In fact, he visited Mary Ann, to ask her to leave her son at school, as he was so able. Mary Ann's pleas to Aubrey to continue his education, were unsuccessful. Reflecting, years later, my father wrote:

> *'Darby,' the Headmaster said, 'It's no use asking you to stay at school, is it? You know it all.' Little did he know how that remark hurt, because a little persuasion at that time would have kept me at school. He made up my mind for me, so I departed with a chip on my shoulder, to make a living full time.*

That chip, in one form or another, stayed with him for the rest of his life. Ironically, he chose to forget that both his headmaster and mother had originally urged him to stay at school, and he had refused. In fairness to him, his school could offer no higher education than he had already received, and his mother could not have afforded grammar school fees. Had he stayed he would have probably become a pupil teacher, and been paid very little.

After the war Aubrey managed to obtain one of the coveted jobs at Electrolux in Luton, where a thriving domestic appliance factory was in its infancy. It was there that he demonstrated his quick grasp of the workings of machinery. With increased confidence, he was soon able to apply for a foreman's job at Bagshawe Conveyors, an iron foundry in Dunstable, and stayed there until he retired, nearly fifty years later.

It was at Electrolux he met Violet West.

A View from the Alley, by A.S. Darby, was published in 1974, by Luton Museum.

Chapter 4: Education and Experience

Towards the end of my father's life I forged a firm relationship with him. Often, in the late 1960s, I would make my way to Luton on a Sunday afternoon to spend several hours listening to snippets of his past. When, however, I asked him awkward questions he clammed up.

He was still writing his book about the back streets of Luton which he had been working on it since I was ten, and thinking about it for many years before that. When he read me extracts I did not dare offer any suggestions or alterations. So fragile was his ego that I feared he would take such comments as insults, or even worse, stop writing altogether.

My father never mentioned his family in his book, apart from his mother. When it was published posthumously, a reader might think that there had only ever been his mother and himself in his family, as his father had disappeared soon after his birth. But his father lived in the marital home until Dad was six, and then lived round the corner. But Aubrey was the youngest of eight siblings, the products of Mary Ann's two marriages. In deciding not to write about them my father was adhering to his maxim: *nothing goes outside the front door*.

One wintry Sunday my father was finally eager to talk. I had made my way from London to Luton through drenching rain. Outside, the wind freshened and howled; my father poked the fire and threw on a few more logs.

'While I was in the army my sister Hettie persuaded Ma to give up her rented house and move in with her. When I came home on leave Ma told me about the plans, but she wasn't keen so I didn't think anything of it.'

I knew very little about the relationship between Hettie and her brother Aubrey, nor would I learn much more. But

39

I was aware that there had been mutual antagonism. Hettie was two years older, and may have resented the close bond between Aubrey and their mother, Mary Ann.

While Aubrey was away in the army Mary Ann lived alone in her little house in a back alley and when he came home on leave he was content to live with her. At twenty-five Aubrey showed no sign of marrying, although he had been courting nineteen-year-old Violet West in a desultory fashion.

Violet decided that she wanted to marry Aubrey Darby, but having a soldier husband was not part of her plan. She suggested that Aubrey should say his mother was very ill and needed her son at home to provide for her. Violet wrote the letter of application herself, and boasted about it in later years. Aubrey signed the letter which asked for his release from the army as his mother desperately needed him at home. She was, he wrote, 'partially blind and had chronic bronchitis,' incapable of work and dependent on her son for income.

It is unlikely that Mary Ann would willingly have condoned the lie, although its morality was not her first consideration, for she was capable of lying to officialdom about the different ages she claimed to be at different times. But it is a mark of her love for her son, and her tolerance, that she allowed herself to be used in this way, for the plan could not have gone ahead without Mary Ann's signature. She was a proud woman, and there is no record of how she felt about being portrayed as a chronically sick, semi-blind old lady.

In fact, Mary Ann lived for another twenty years and worked for most of them as a housekeeper. Although she was a heavy smoker, even at eighty she was capable of sprinting daily for the bus, berating the driver for arriving too early.

My father never spoke of his early exit from the army. He might well have felt regretful, as his discharge papers record that he would have made a good non-commissioned officer. The papers also show that he was slight: five foot six and one hundred and thirty pounds. In weight, height and looks he was almost identical to the father he despised.

The most significant fact about the whole episode is that Aubrey Darby allowed Violet West to manipulate him. Even so, at this stage Aubrey was in no hurry to marry, despite pressure from Violet. She longed to be married and have a home of her own. Then Aubrey's circumstances suddenly changed: the day he finally left the army he arrived home to find that Hettie had moved their mother out the day before. The keys had been returned to the landlord and my father's few possessions were in a neat pile on the pavement by the front door.

'To be fair to Hettie, perhaps she was thinking of Ma,' said Dad. 'Our house was practically a slum in the worst area of the town, down an alley just off Chase Street. And my belongings weren't up to much otherwise they'd have been pinched overnight.'

We both laughed. As a child I had become familiar with his comment when the house was in a mess: 'This bloody place looks like Chase Street,' but I had never known that Chase Street had once existed.

I looked at him. He was gazing into the fire and I realised that there was more to the story than a daughter offering her mother a home. I waited.

'Hettie was proud of her smart semi in Dunstable. Her husband, Cyril, had a good job and they were buying their house. Most people rented in those days.'

As my father reflected for longer, his tone became bitter. 'Oh yes, Hettie acted the loving daughter all right. She was the one to give notice to Ma's landlord and pack up Ma's few bits and pieces. It gave her great joy to put my things in the street. When I came home the pair of them had hopped it to Dunstable and the door was locked.'

'What did you do, Dad?'

'I went straight over to your mother's house and told her we'd get married as soon as possible, and we did, a few weeks later. I found a job at Bagshawe Conveyors in Dunstable and a house to rent in Dunstable High Street.'

Violet - aged 19, Aubrey - aged 25 1931

'What was the wedding like, Dad? Did Mum have an engagement ring?' I had wondered that before as I had never seen one on her finger, just a cheap gold band biting into it.

'I bought her a diamond solitaire with a matching wedding ring. When times got hard we pawned it and could never afford the redemption fee. As to the wedding,' – he broke off and his face darkened. Leaning forward he made a great show of kicking a log which hung over the edge of the fender threatening to dislodge its ash over the hearth rug.

'Your mother's brother Jim turned up, and so did her mother. No one came from my side of the family. We were married on the Saturday and went back to work on Monday morning. When we got home from work that evening there was a large parcel of linen on the doorstep. There was no label, no card, but I knew that my mother had left it there, a wedding gift.'

'Linen? Sheets and towels?'

He nodded. 'Yes, all excellent quality. My mother liked good linen. It lasted years.'

'Did you go to see her and thank her, Dad?'

His eyes flashed in their customary way. 'Go to Hettie's house? You've got to be bloody joking. But my mother moved back to Luton later, and got a job housekeeping for Boss Horn - well that's how she always referred to him.' He chuckled at the memory. 'Sometimes I went to see her there. Took some of the children over. It was before your time.'

Then his expression sobered. 'I couldn't go much. Violet didn't like her mother-in-law. And she hated Hettie.'

My father coughed and spat into the back of the fire. I avoided looking at the hissing phlegm and finally said, That's understandable I suppose, if they were hostile to her.'

'My mother wasn't hostile, but she did what Hettie told her to do.'

I reflected on the spirited Mary Ann, a fighter and opportunist for most of her life, finally succumbing to her stronger daughter's will. I felt sad.

'Anyway,' said my father, 'we had a good time when we were first married, your mother and me. She had never been to the seaside, and I took her there on a day trip.' He gazed into the whispering heat. 'I'll always remember her face when she saw the sea for the first time.'

I remembered a letter Shirley, living in America, had received from him. He had written:

It is late at night. I am on my own in the house, surrounded by ghosts, but they are all friendly.

I wondered if the ghosts were always with him.

My father suddenly had an abrupt change of mood, his pensiveness shattered, his tone bemused.

'There we were in our house in Dunstable High Street, both with good jobs, enjoying life, and your mother gets herself pregnant.'

I looked at him, startled. There was no trace of irony in his expression.

'You weren't ready for children?' I chose my words carefully.

'I didn't want *any* bloody children. But, if we had to have any, four would have been a reasonable number, a maximum number.'

He was telling this to his sixth child.

Suddenly my father decided he'd said enough. 'Go and put the kettle on gal. Make it nice and strong. None of your piss.'

As I made my way back to London that evening, I thought about my father's story. I wondered whether Hettie had been acting less out of malice, and more out of concern for her mother. Perhaps she had guessed the reasons Dad had given for leaving the army and had been appalled at the way Mary Ann's name had been exploited.

I started to think about what had followed the birth of the first child, a boy, Anthony John. My mother was delighted with her son, as she was when Shirley Ann arrived two years later. But more children followed in quick succession, and she found it increasingly hard to cope.

My mother had a mercurial personality. She could be both cruel and compassionate. Shirley remembers that I was born with bandy legs, and was prescribed splints, to be worn at night, to straighten them. My mother could not bear listening to my distress at the discomfort, and soon stopped using them.

She found it easy to leave the children in her frenzy of socialising, and was happy for her two eldest children to assume a dangerous level of responsibility. As soon as Tony and Shirley were old enough to wash and dress themselves, they had helped with their younger brothers and sisters. The family had moved twice by this time, and was living at 322 Luton Road. For Shirley, in particular, life was hard. By the time she was ten there were four children younger than her, and most of her time was spent looking after them.

Shirley remembered one incident as particularly painful. She was ten and it was a school day. She stood at the kitchen sink, gazing out of the window, across the back garden. Her fingers played with the suds in the washing up water. On the left side of the garden she could see the thriving vegetable patch: beans, cabbages, carrots, potatoes. My father won prizes at the local produce show, held annually at Evelyn Road School, round the corner. To his fury, my mother refused to cook these vegetables as he used chicken manure to help their growth. When Dad tried to explain about the wider use of manure in farming, she looked at him with contempt. 'You think I was born yesterday. Of course they don't use animal droppings, so don't talk such disgusting filth. '

Dad picked his beautiful crop; Mum gave it away directly he was out of sight, then bought inferior vegetables from the corner shop.

The right side of the garden was the domain of the chickens, and Shirley could see them strutting and busy.

At the bottom of the garden was Back Field, a strip of grass, rich with clover, from which the children sucked the sweetness, pretending it was sugar. Cheerful with scabious and dog daisies, proud with buttercups, the field skirted the row of houses between Belle Vue Garage and the Halfway House Hotel. The children in the houses gathered there to play. And the other side of Back Field was the playground of Evelyn Road School. The shouts and laughter of the children in the dinner- time break enticed her, but Shirley knew that there was no hope of joining them.

'Shirley,' her mother's voice broke into her thoughts. 'Have you finished the washing-up?'

'Nearly, Mum.' Hastily Shirley emptied the dirty water down the sink, and grabbed the tea towel to begin drying the dishes.

'Then bring me a cup of tea, and don't forget to rinse the cup with boiling water.'

A loud knock at the front door interrupted proceedings. 'Shirley, see who that is.'

Obediently Shirley dried her hands and opened the door to find an officious looking man, complete with brief-case, on the step.

'Mum, it's a gentleman.' She raised her voice so her mother could hear in the living room.

'I don't want to buy anything. Say, "No thank you," and close the door.'

The man looked irritated and shuffled his feet. He cleared his throat and called down the hall, 'Mrs. Darby, I have just come from a meeting with Miss Greenwood, at Evelyn Road School. I wish to discuss your daughter's attendance.'

A moment's silence, then, 'Shirley, invite the gentleman in, and then make him a nice cup of tea. Don't forget the saucer.' As the man entered the living room Mum gave a tinkling laugh. 'You know what children are like, I'm sure. They do lack social graces. Now, how can I help you? Shirley, close the door after you. The gentleman and I need to discuss matters that are no business of children.'

Shirley knew what 'don't forget the saucer meant' and so ran next door to borrow two matching cups and saucers from Mrs. Coombes. Back in the kitchen, Shirley skipped and jumped. She realised that the visitor was the truancy officer, and that it meant that she would be going back to school. It was nearly a month since she had last run round the corner to join her friends at Evelyn Road. It had begun with Mum being unwell and staying home from work for a few days. Shirley had felt despairing as she knew what would happen. It always did. She was kept at home to look after her mother while the other children went to school and nursery as usual. This time, when Mum returned to work, Jill caught a heavy cold, and so Shirley had to continue staying at home to look after her. Then, as Jill recovered, Shirley herself was crippled with pains in her back, and cried as she dragged herself out of bed in the morning.

'It's your kidneys,' said her mother, not without sympathy, 'You take after me.'

'Growing pains,' said her father, 'Work it off.'

As her mother hurried out of the door to work, she said, 'If you're not going to school, you can take Jill and Judy to nursery. That will save Tony a job. If you still feel ill after that, you can go back to bed.'

Coming back down the hill from the nursery the pain became stronger; Shirley gasped and bent double. A kindly neighbour stopped to ask if she was all right. 'It's growing pains,' explained Shirley, 'I'm going to work it off,' and she struggled through the garden gate on her way to bed.

The attack passed after a few days, but her mother said it would be a good idea if she took longer off school. After all, it had been a nasty bout and she could stay in the warm and get some housework done.

'Please let me go to school,' said Shirley, 'I don't want to stay at home.'

There was no discussion. Shirley stayed off school, and was still running the home when her mother had another of her bad heads and vomiting. Although she could probably look after herself at these times, Shirley knew there was the extra complication of Mum fearing her own company, something never voiced.

The truancy officer's visit coincided with the last day of her mother's illness. She was due to return to work the next day, but no one had mentioned Shirley being allowed to go back to school.

So, for Shirley, the visit was a miracle. The man would tell Mum she was wrong, and that Shirley must go back to her lessons.

Nudging the door open with her foot, Shirley entered the living room, carefully balancing the cups of tea. To her surprise, Mum and the man were laughing and talking like old friends.

The man turned to Shirley. 'So you're Mummy's helper. I hear what a good girl you are to help your mother with the little ones. It's so difficult for Mummy never being able to go out with her poor health. How old are you?' He consulted his file and gave Mum a reassuring smile. Shirley watched anxiously. 'Ten years old, and quite the mother. Mummy is so proud of you, doing all the things she can't, but would love to do.'

A shiver ran down Shirley's back as she realised that this man was not going to help her go back to school. He was still talking to her in a patronising tone: 'And your older brother is doing so well at the grammar school - passed the scholarship a year early. But girls are the future homemakers, aren't they? It's so hard for your mother, who would so love to be strong and run the home without help.'

Shirley looked at Mum, and caught her giving the truancy officer a gentle, wistful smile. 'How well you understand,' Mum murmured.

The man leaned forward, and said earnestly, 'Mrs. Darby, keep Shirley home whenever you need her. I fully understand.'

Shirley wanted to cry, but knew better. Mum would say, 'Stop that crying, or I'll give you something to cry for.' With a cold resignation she realised that her hopes of going to school regularly had gone. Even the truancy officer wouldn't help her.

It was some days after the truancy officer's visit that Shirley eventually returned to school. Shy at first and wary of the curiosity about her long absence, she kept her head down and concentrated on her lessons. Mum had told her she must say that she had been suffering from 'flu with complications' if anyone asked. But soon she relaxed, enjoying the familiar routine of the classroom and the chalk-laden atmosphere. Even the odour of the stale, unwashed bodies of children was not unwelcome, and she revelled in the predictability of the day.

As the children lined up after lunch-time play, a whisper spread down the line: 'Nitty Nora's here.' And sure enough the children were told to form an orderly queue in the corridor to have their heads checked for lice.

Standing next to a table which carried a bowl of disinfectant stood a tall, angular lady with a mouth like a rat-trap. No one had ever seen Nitty Nora smile. Her wire wool hair was scraped back viciously from her face into a severe bun. Not a trace of make-up softened the rough red features, and her eyes were as cold as the charity she lacked. She would dip what looked remarkably like a knitting needle into the bowl of disinfectant, trawl through a child's hair, give a grunt of dissatisfaction if she found nothing, then give a sharp nudge to the child's back. The victim would stumble away, and she would claw another forward. When Nitty Nora found evidence of infestation she would dig her bony fingers triumphantly into the child's shoulders and march the cringing pupil down the corridor like a criminal to Miss Greenwood, the headmistress.

Shirley waited anxiously, relieved when she received the push in her back that meant her head was clear. But three children were not so lucky and Miss Greenwood sent home letters to all the parents that afternoon, warning them that any child found with head lice would be banned from school until a doctor's note confirmed that the situation had been dealt with properly. Miss Greenwood accepted the common convention that head lice were caused by lack of hygiene.

When Mum read the letter explaining the anti head infestation procedure, she reacted strongly. 'No child of mine gets head lice. My children's heads are clean. It's disgusting that people send their children to school with filthy vermin crawling in their hair, ready to infest others.'

She became alarmed when Shirley told her that the three infested children were in Shirley's class. There had been no attempt to keep their identity secret, and a long line of children had watched their ignominious trek down to Miss Greenwood's room, marshalled by a self-satisfied Nitty Nora. There was an air of black comedy about it all. Miss Greenwood had responded to the knock on her door, by coming into the corridor and closing the door firmly behind her. Her look of distaste was profound. No bugs were to have the chance to infiltrate *her* room, and she stood several feet away from the luckless children, who by now were weeping wrecks. Within seconds the children had been despatched home with Mrs. Greenwood's voice ringing down the corridor, 'Tell your mothers a letter will be in the post by the end of the afternoon with clear instructions what they must do.'

Mum was terrified of such disgrace, and Shirley tried to console her. 'Mum, it's all right, I haven't got nits.'

'But the eggs might have been too tiny for the nurse to see. You probably played with the children who have got nits. That would be typical. You didn't, did you?' Mum's voice rose in alarm.

We all believed Mum could read our minds and so Shirley confessed that one of them was a friend with whom she had played two-ball that morning.

We waited anxiously, knowing all too well that Mum's mood changes came out of the blue, and weren't surprised when she went white and her fists clenched. 'You stupid little cow, now you're bound to get them. Wait till your father gets home.'

Tony looked up from his homework with a quizzical expression on his face. 'I can't see Dad going barmy about it like you. He'll probably say that there are more important things to worry about and just to wait and see what happens.'

His mother gave only an absent minded swipe in Tony's direction for his cheek for she was absorbing the truth of what he had said. 'You're right. He won't be any help. I've got to think of something myself.'

All went quiet, and then she snapped her fingers triumphantly. 'I know - paraffin.'

Tony looked apprehensive. 'What do you mean? What are you going to do with paraffin?'

'Don't be bloody stupid, I'm going to use it to clean Shirley's head.'

As Shirley backed away into a corner Tony said, 'Mum, be reasonable, say you're joking. You can't pour paraffin over Shirley's head. What will you do then - set light to her?'

His mother gave her tinkling laugh as at a joke. Tony assumed all was well and returned to his homework. Shirley watched Mum warily and kept out of her way, making sure that she did all her household chores so carefully that she couldn't arouse her anger. Never had the table been set with such precision, or the kitchen floor washed so thoroughly.

Shortly before his father came home Tony went out to feed the chickens.

'Quick, Shirley, come here.' Mum grabbed the can of paraffin from under the sink. 'Put your head over the bowl before Tony comes back and makes trouble by telling your father.' She glared at Jill and me as we peered round the corner from the back room. 'Get back in there and play quietly. It's nearly your bedtime.'

We backed away, fearful of being sent to bed earlier than necessary, but listened wide-eyed and scared to Shirley's begging.

'Please, Mum, no. I haven't got nits, I haven't. Nitty Nora said so.'

Mum gripped Shirley's arm and hauled her towards the sink. 'I'm doing this for you. Do you want the other children to despise you when those eggs hatch? Do you want your mother disgraced by being one of those children with nitty hair?' She shuddered. 'I couldn't bear the shame.'

Shirley put her head over the sink. The cold paraffin gushed over her head, and the fumes made her choke and retch.

'Mum, I feel sick, I'm going to faint.'

'Keep your eyes closed then you'll be all right,' said Mum, one eye on the back door as she swilled the paraffin haphazardly over Shirley. 'That should do it. Stop crying or I'll give you something to cry for. Here, dry your face and neck with this towel,' and she flung the dirty scrap of worn cloth which served as a kitchen-do-all towards a sobbing Shirley. Her face and neck rapidly became red and raw, and Mum applied Nivea cream before Shirley went to bed.

'No need to mention it to your father, ' she said, 'and I've told Tony to keep his mouth shut.'

'I'm so sore, Mum,' said Shirley, 'and my head hurts.'

'You'll feel better in the morning, and just think you won't be one of those dirty children with nits.'

The next morning Shirley woke with a throbbing head and a blistered face and neck. Even her mother was worried when she saw that Shirley's head was noticeably swollen with weeping sores. She couldn't put a comb through her hair without crying out in pain.

'Crikey Mum,' said Tony, 'Shirley's head has grown enormous. She looks like a monster. You'll have to take her to the doctor.'

'No need,' said my mother, the tinkling laugh in evidence again, a sign she was nervous. 'She'll be as right as rain in a few days' time. A couple of days at home will do the trick. There's a few jobs to catch up on round the house, so that's a bonus. I'll send a note in by one of the others to say she's got a cold. We don't want them thinking she's got nits.'

Although my mother often kept Shirley away from school, Tony was never asked to stay at home. At Evelyn Road his promise was recognised early on. For the first few years of the war, schooling was interrupted, and classes went in for half a day only, so the London evacuees could be accommodated. But as the school got back to normal, Miss Greenwood, the head teacher, suggested to my parents that Tony should take the scholarship for grammar school a year early. It was rare before the 1944 Education Act that a working class boy would even attempt the examination, for even if he had passed, who would pay the fees? The Act revolutionised education for the working classes as it provided free places at grammar schools for all those who could pass the eleven plus examination.

Miss Greenwood believed Tony could pass the examination and told our parents. My father explained that there was nothing he would like better for his son, but said he doubted if he could afford the fees.

'Mr. Darby, there are two types of scholarship, pass to pay, and a few places for pass with the tuition paid for: if Tony should pass at that level you only provide uniform and equipment. Could you manage that?'

My father didn't hesitate. A wonderful new world dawned for his son. Tony would have the education he had dreamed of for himself. Through Tony he would fulfil his own thwarted ambitions. I don't think our mother saw it in quite the same way. She was just bursting to tell the neighbours that Miss Greenwood thought that Tony was exceptionally bright. The story became embellished with each telling.

Tony duly sat the examination after months of his father sitting over him, coaching him, shouting and thumping if he thought his son was proving stupid or idle. At school the coaching was rigorous but fair. Miss Moss, who took the top class, the oldest children, had an acerbic tongue, and was ruthless with the idle, but she was an excellent teacher who encouraged Tony. 'You are a scholar,' she said, 'and must live up to that.'

Miss Greenwood agreed, but added that Tony was successful because he worked so hard. 'Shirley is a natural scholar,' she told our mother, 'and if allowed, will go right to the top.' However, although our father did want a good education for all his family, by now he realised that his wife could not manage without Shirley's frequent absences from school to look after the younger children. Life at home was often traumatic, and he was fast getting to the stage where he ignored Shirley's treatment in a desperate, unsuccessful attempt to keep peace.

My mother came home from Open Day and relayed her conversation with Miss Greenwood to my father, proud that another of her children was also being commended. Dad looked at her, a slight frown knitting his already heavily lined forehead.

'What did she mean by that? What was she implying by 'allowed'?'

My mother gave an airy wave of her fingers.

'It's just words, Dabber, just words. You analyse things too much.'

My father sighed, and turned his attention to coaching Tony. There were only a few days left, and he thought that Tony was nowhere near the standard required, without knowing what that standard was.

As soon as my father reached home on the day of the tests, he interrogated Tony in great detail. 'So you think the English went well? Did you start your essay with a quotation like I told you to? What was the essay title? Which quotation from the ones we prepared did you use? Are you sure that was the most appropriate? What about the Maths? Did you finish all the questions?'

Tony was honest and misguided enough to confess that he had only managed half of the last question before the time had run out.

'You stupid bloody fool. How do you think you're going to pass? That's it, you've failed.' Eyes blazing, Dad retreated behind his paper, only emerging at intervals to give Tony a contemptuous glance. For weeks afterwards he would mutter every time Tony was in earshot, 'Halfa, Arthur who? Arthurquestion.'

Then the letter arrived. Subject to an interview, Tony had won a free scholarship to Dunstable School as a day boy.

'Don't know how you managed that, when you only did half the last question. The rest of the candidates must have been idiots.'

'Leave him alone, Dabber. You know you don't mean it. I'm really proud of you, Tony.' And his mother hurried off to break the news to the neighbours, carefully omitting the small matter of the interview.

More practice sessions, this time in interview techniques.

'Look them straight in the eye. Stand upright. Address them as 'Sir or Madam.'

'There won't be any women interviewing me, Dad. Miss Greenwood says there are no women at the school except the matron and the headmaster's wife.'

'Don't bloody cheek me. They might include a woman to throw you off guard.'

If ten year-old Tony thought that it was impossible for any woman to throw him, after living with his mother, he was wise enough to keep quiet.

'Now, hobbies.' His father frowned. 'You've got to have some academic hobbies. You already read a lot, so that's one, but they'll want to know what kind of books you read. We've only got a fortnight so you read a history book a night, starting with *The Life and Times of Queen Victoria.*'

Each evening after school, Tony was told to listen to the Home Service for several hours until his father was satisfied that he knew sufficient about current affairs. He taught him the policies and philosophies of the main political parties, and urged Tony not to tell the interviewing panel that his father had strong Socialist beliefs.

'People like that, people with money and status, wouldn't approve,' he said vaguely. 'They want you to conform. The time to stick your neck out is when you go to university. At that stage they teach you to break down accepted principles.'

Tony probably had no idea what our father meant, but over the years we all became used to him speaking in a foreign language, and he said nothing.

Dunstable School was famous for its sporting record, and our father thought there would be questions about sport. Here Tony was more assured, and stood up well to the battery of questions shot at him.

The day of the interview my father hauled Tony from his bed at 6 am. 'You'll need hours to get yourself looking halfway decent.'

Tony was allowed the rare privilege of a bath, but so the water shouldn't be wasted all the children were immersed in quick succession afterwards. We must have bemused about having a bath on a weekday.

Tony had polished his shoes the night before to his father's exacting standards, and now, in starched white shirt, his father's best tie and Brylcreemed hair slicked back, he looked shiny, smart and uncomfortable. At last his father was satisfied and with a few last minute words of advice – 'Remember to stand up straight, shake hands firmly, look them in the eye, thank them for their time' – he disappeared out the back door to cycle to work.

Tony enjoyed the interview, finding it much easier than any practice ones his father had subjected him to, and came home reasonably confident. The headmaster had told him he was looking forward to welcoming him into the school in September. When the final letter arrived, saying that Tony's place at the school was now assured, his father allowed himself a smile.

'Well done, boy, I knew you'd do it,' was his only comment, but he bought Tony an Oxford dictionary, which lived in the bookcase for many years, consulted on a daily basis by at least one Darby child grappling with homework. I found my father a quicker, more succinct dictionary though, and used him regularly.

'What's vindicated mean, Dad?' I asked one day, reading from the headlines of the newspaper which absorbed him.

'Proved right,' he said, without looking up, and later, when I checked, I could understand his definition more easily than the convoluted dictionary version: *maintain the cause of person, religion etc successfully...*

As it happened our father had one year to pay for Tony's text books for the 1944 Education Act freed him from that burden, and paved the way for the rest of his children to be able to sit the 11+ examination without fear that the money could not be found for the required books. In our house the examination continued to be termed 'the scholarship' mainly because that was what Miss Greenwood and Miss Moss called it.

Tony loved Dunstable Grammar School, as it became after 1944, but fitting his responsibilities at home into the exacting academic demands proved difficult. One of his chores was to cook the chicken mash after school, let it cool, and then feed the chickens. He arrived home late one winter's day, after rugby practice, and ladled the mash, still hot and steaming, into the chicken troughs. The chickens had given up on their meal when it grew dark and had already roosted. A tremendous squawking echoed round the garden.

'Shut up you stupid birds, and eat your food,' said Tony, panic stricken that his father would arrive home any second and see that they hadn't been fed at the correct time. That would mean a good hiding. Tony knew that

Shirley would have fed the younger ones and put them to bed, also that she would not tell tales, so it was simply a matter of racing the clock.

Although the chickens came before sports' practice, our father encouraged Tony's love of rugby and cricket, and in his son's early days at Dunstable Grammar, would go along to the matches to cheer him on. As a boy Dad had dreamed of a career in professional football until a broken leg, at the age of sixteen, ended that ambition. His only satisfaction came from playing for his firm's football team on Saturdays, until Mum's complaining also stopped that.

Tony still shared Shirley's burden of caring for their young brothers and sisters. Frequently the household was in chaos, and he always remembered the shame of opening the back door to find a school friend there, asking to borrow a textbook. The boy looked past Tony into the kitchen, at the pile of dirty dishes, and a baby sitting in the middle of the floor in a smelly nappy, screaming in distress from sheer neglect for it was all too much for Tony and Shirley to manage efficiently. A toddler stood beside Tony, with a face smeared in jam.

'Oh my God,' said the boy in disdain, and turned on his heel without repeating his request for the book. At school the next day Tony was aware of giggling and nose holding. He silenced his tormentors in the only way he knew, by making them suffer on the rugby field and beating them in class tests.

Shirley's turn came to sit the scholarship. The problem of buying text books had been removed as she took the examination after 1944. However, money problems did not loom as large in the Darby family by this time, as our mother was continuing to earn good money.

How Shirley achieved her place at grammar school, The Cedars, in Leighton Buzzard, is difficult to assess. She passed the examination with a skeletal education, and also had to outstrip the boys. Girls had to score more highly than boys for it was realised by the educational theorists of the time that eleven-year-old girls were more advanced than boys of the same age.

There was no extra coaching for Shirley, and no attempts to step up her attendance in that vital year before the examination. This was the beginning of Dad's desire to see his children educated well slowly eroding over the years as domestic problems and traumas gained greater significance.

When I was ten, in my preparation for the scholarship, Miss Greenwood sent home letters to all the parents. Miss Moss would be setting the top class homework, for the first time in the school's history, so that we would get plenty of practice for the examination. Parents were asked to sign the permission slip at the bottom of the letter. In his almost illegible bold copperplate, Dad wrote across the slip:

This examination is supposed to be a test of natural intelligence.

Judith will not be doing the homework.

Years later I commented to my brother Roger, that, embarrassing as it had been for me to be the only child in the class not given homework, I had to admire Dad's principles. Roger laughed:

'Don't be silly. The sub text read, "there's washing up to be done and the chickens to feed. Judith won't have time to do homework." '

The school summer holidays of 1946 brought Tony and Shirley the usual relief from the stress of term time. The worry of getting the younger ones ready before school was over for a few weeks and caring for them was growing easier. I was the youngest, and would be three that November, Jill was five and had started school at Easter. We were quiet children and did as Shirley bade.

Roy, seven, and Roger, nine, could virtually look after themselves, and if they disobeyed him, Tony dealt with them in the only way he knew, from the example he had learned from his father. In later years that memory grieved him terribly.

Life looked good. Our parents had two weeks off when the factories closed down for a fortnight. We didn't go away on holiday, very few people did at that time, but Dad would play impromptu games of football and cricket with the older children in Back Field, and find time to play cards and Monopoly. Somehow he always managed to buy one of everything on the board, ensuring a stalemate which only he could control.

The tension which gripped the household in term time was released. Each day I played with Jill and her friends Marion and Gillian. Jill always made friends easily and if I wanted to tag along I knew I must be quiet and do as I was told. Only Michael Brown was my age in that row of houses, and his mother considered him too young to be allowed out to play. Gillian's father stored sacks of onions in various stages of rotting in his garden shed, and we sometimes gathered in there to chew them, with stomachs of cast iron. With hunger never far away, we considered them a delicacy.

Our parents returned to work and the reins of the household were taken up again by Tony and Shirley. Left alone, we children took risks. Playing too recklessly in the chalk pits, Shirley tumbled from top to bottom, and landed shaken and bruised. She limped home and told us we were not to tell Mum or Dad, for at the very least it would mean a telling-off and a ban on the chalk pits.

On another morning, in that long summer holiday, Tony was kicking a ball aimlessly round the back garden when nine-year-old Keithy Lewis from next door, urinated on him from his upstairs bedroom window. Tony shouted out in disgust, then jumped over the fence, wrenched open the back door, and pounded up the stairs. He punched the snivelling Keithy and warned him what he would do if the trick was tried again.

'You are a disgusting oaf,' said Tony, and rubbed his urine soaked jumper in Keithy's face.

Keithy scream grew louder.

'It stinks, it stinks, get it away from me.'

'It's your pee,' yelled Tony, 'here, have another sniff.'

That evening there was a knock on the door, and my father opened it to Mr. Lewis. Red-faced and furious, Mr. Lewis stuck his fist in my father's face and spat out:

'Your bully-boy bloody son beat up my Keithy this morning, and rubbed pee into his face.'

Next to his father, secure in his protection, Keithy smirked. My father made no comment about the fact that Keithy was already taller and fatter than Tony, but called to Tony to the door.

Tony had no fear of Mr. Lewis or Keithy, but he trembled as he wondered what his father would do or say. He spoke out honestly.

'Yes, I did hit him, Dad, and I did rub his face in his own pee. He peed on me out of his bedroom window.'

'Then you did right, son.'

Turning away from Tony, and back to Mr. Lewis, my father said,

'I think you need to teach your son the basic decencies of life. How did you expect Tony to react? You can't put an old head on young shoulders. He's only eleven for God's sake. Goodbye.'

My father shut the door before Mr. Lewis could draw breath. Tony waited in the back room, anxious to know if there would be punishment after the public show of support. But all his father said, was, 'Keep out of the firing line of the dirty little bastard in future.'

We children were happy during the holidays. The early morning chaos of term-time was eased, although Tony and Shirley still had full responsibility for the care of the younger ones. As the war drew to an end it was less common for mothers of small children to go out to work. Those that did relied on older brothers and sisters to look after the younger ones, but it was rare for them to do the amount of housework that Shirley did. The rows between our parents were not so frequent with the less stressful pace of life, but mainly because our father had learned to avoid confrontation. When the rows did erupt, however, they shattered the whole household. It was hard to see what the rows were about, but often it was due to sheer boredom and malice on my mother's part. Once started, she wanted to keep the momentum going and followed my father all round the house, provoking, sneering, shouting, giving him no peace. Frequently he would take himself to bed just to escape the endless nagging, but she would follow him up to the bedroom.

Lying two up and two down in one bed, we youngest children shrank from the vicious altercations which came through the dividing wall. Clinging to Roy's leg with one hand, stuffing the army blanket into my mouth with the other, I chewed away at the edging. Jill was as terrified as I was, but Roy allowed me to keep clinging on to him, and Roger would turn over in the cramped space and mutter, 'It will all be over soon.'

'What have you got to say for yourself? Are you a man or a mouse? Just run away when I'm talking to you. Well you can't escape because I'm right here, and here I'm staying.' It seemed to me that it would never be over.

Finally, my father would leap from the bed and hit Mum hard, round the face. She would dissolve into noisy, triumphant tears, and we children, though shocked and anxious for her welfare, would realise that this was the end of this particular episode.

It was my mother's unpredictability that raised the anxiety in our home. I longed for everyone always to be happy and smiling, and from very early on would pray that Mum and Dad would not row. I vowed that if harmony could be achieved between them, then I would never ask for anything else. I have taken such childish prayers into adulthood, silently uttering them in times of distress.

Chapter 5: Abortion and Adoption

In 1945 abortion was illegal in England. If Violet and her friends had an unwanted pregnancy they usually resigned themselves to having the baby. There was no shortage of advice about the unwanted condition. Copious amounts of gin and a hot bath, extreme exercise, castor oil, were all variously tried, but usually failed. There were other foul concoctions, also, dispensed by local illegal quacks, which were ill-advised and dangerous. For the desperate, there were back street abortions, performed by untrained individuals, usually women.

If she was unmarried a woman might be pushed into marriage with the often reluctant father, or if she could bear the neighbours' stigma and whispering, she could raise the child as an unmarried mother. To do that she invariably needed parental support.

Another solution was to have the baby adopted.

Contraception was still very unreliable in the 1940s. Many women still saw abstinence as the best way of limiting pregnancy. There were contraceptive jellies and condoms available, and also pessaries, but nothing was reliable.

In the summer of 1945, street parties were at their height. Celebration was everywhere, and an air of recklessness. Even rationing became bearable now peace was finally here.

Our parents met their friends most evenings in a congenial pub, *The Red Lion,* and the household stumbled along, run by Tony and Shirley. My father thought the worst was over. All the children were now at school or nursery, and he could imagine a time when all his children would be old enough to help run the home, and life would be worry-free. When Roger and Roy weren't at school they were outside playing with their friends, Roger leading and dominating, Roy falling in with what was planned. Jill and I would be packed off to bed immediately after tea, and family life was as reasonable as was possible in the Darby household.

Then Violet realised that she was pregnant once more. The experience of six previous pregnancies meant she knew beyond doubt that she was carrying another child. The terrible nausea and vomiting she always suffered as soon as she conceived, mocked her, assuring her that several months of suffering lay ahead. The experience of my birth and her pneumonia was still sharp and clear in her memory, and her immediate feeling was one of dread. Aubrey was appalled, too. For him, the memory of the financial crisis which had followed my birth was uppermost. He was a man who had never wanted children, who admitted to finding babies irksome and boring, who could see that pregnancy and childbirth were eroding his wife's health. I do not know in what order all those thoughts came to his mind, but I do know he was relieved that my mother also did not want a child.

My mother acted swiftly. Her friend Sylvia knew a backstreet abortionist, Mrs. Smith, who was reputed to be cheap, gentle and painless. She was a close friend of Mum's brother Jim. Grandma West didn't approve of Mrs. Smith, and never referred to her by her first name. Grandma didn't know Mrs. Smith's trade, but was suspicious of her over-painted looks and tight clothes, her beer drinking - 'in pint glasses, Violet, she's not a lady' – and her brash confidence. Grandma tried to convince herself that Jim was just a friend to Mrs. Smith. After all, he was on good terms with Mr. Smith, so nothing could be 'going on', could it? There was another fear which Grandma confided only to her daughter. The Smiths had a son, whom the neighbours described as Jim's double.

My mother tried to reassure Grandma, and laughed. 'People say all sorts of things that aren't true. Don't worry about it. And don't let Dabber hear you say such things, you know he hates gossip.'

Grandma was not a gossip: she said no more.

Sylvia made an appointment with Mrs. Smith, from which my mother came home sobbing, her face like cracked marble. Holding on to the bannister for support, bent double, she dragged herself up the stairs. Tony and Shirley watched silently. The days leading up to this had been traumatic for the whole family. We had listened to her being sick, and crying that she didn't want another baby. Neither Shirley nor Tony knew what an abortion was, and that word had not been mentioned in front of us. We had no understanding of why she was now so stricken. Halfway up the stairs Violet turned and looked down at Shirley.

'When your father comes home, tell him I'm in bed. Tell him how ill I am, and tell him he's to come nowhere near me, ever again.'

'Where's your mother?' Dad ran through the back door after work. Shirley repeated the message, and he took the stairs two at a time. Through the closed bedroom door came our mother's muffled voice, rising in angry reproach, and his, measured and placating. Then heavy sobs and wails from Mum, like keening. At the bottom of the stairs Tony and Shirley looked at each other, bewildered and scared.

'What's happened, Tony?'

'I'm not sure, but I don't think there's going to be a baby.

A short while later Dad came down and put on the kettle, an unusual occurrence. Putting his hand in his pocket he pulled out a handful of coins. 'Tony, run to Chorleys for some aspirin, and then to the off-licence for half a bottle of brandy. Be quick about it.'

Dad's hand shook as he counted out the money, and his face was grey under the foundry grime. As Tony ran out through the door, Dad seemed to notice Shirley for the first time. 'Don't look like that, Shirley. Your mother is going to be all right.'

Violet made a rapid physical recovery, but it was some weeks before she wanted to socialise again. Then, the familiar pattern re-asserted itself, and her depression lifted. Getting ready to go out in the evening she would laugh and chatter, teasing Dad, flirting with him, rousing him from lethargy at the end of his working day. Our father felt the tension leave him, and humoured his wife. Yet when his black moods descended, there was no humouring, and even she became scared.

Both parents had mood swings but Dad's were usually dependent on Mum's. If she was in good spirits then he generally was too. As the years went by the whole household responded to her state of mind, and could be sunk in fear and depression or raised to levels of happiness and excitement.

It hadn't always been so. In the days when Dad was the sole earner he used that as a weapon, and would sit reading his newspaper on a Friday evening, oblivious to his wife's pleas for some housekeeping. It wasn't until her tears, begging and rage grew too much for him to ignore that he would put his hand in his pocket and bring out his wage packet. This perverse streak never went away. Many years later, as a widower, he would invite the insurance agent in on a Friday evening and keep him sitting there for up to two hours before handing over the weekly payment. I could never understand why the agent put up with such treatment but frequently he laughed and said his Friday visit was better than going to the pictures, and a bonus was that one of us would always make him a cup of tea.

Dad's black moods were terrifying. We all kept away, as the slightest careless word could result in a bashing. As 1946 drew to a close the household became tense. Dad was quiet, a bad sign. Perhaps he was angry that Mum had overspent at Christmas, and he was worried about debt. Maybe there were problems at work, maybe he lived in fear of another pregnancy, but usually there was nothing obvious to explain his intermittent rage, except for the occasions when Mum deliberately drove him to fury. I would bite my nails to the quick and draw blood, or chew away cuffs or skirt hems as I crouched in a corner, holding my breath, watching and fearing as my mother's volatile mood swiftly moved from happy and generous through to vicious and vengeful. I felt it was important to stay out of the way in case someone blamed me. At those times all my siblings became silent and watchful, trying to make themselves invisible.

Bottles of spirits bought for Christmas were now half empty, and Mum had grouped them on a small table in the corner of the front room. Our parents were still at work although Dad was due home any minute. Shirley ran round, tidying frantically. In the hall Roger kicked a ball.

'Stop that Roger, Dad will be home in a minute.

Roger kicked the ball through the front room door. The bottles smashed to the ground. At that moment Dad walked through the back door.

Although terrified, Roger didn't hesitate. 'Dad, Dad, Shirley kicked the ball, and look what she's done.'

Roger's was the first voice our father heard, and he listened to no other. Tongue between his teeth, he grabbed Shirley and thrashed her. Sobbing, she crouched in the corner, and as her father's eyes once more took in the broken bottles and glasses, his fury mounted again. Roy's toy metal train, a Christmas present, was lying in the middle of the floor. Dad hurled it at Shirley, and a sharp edge caught her lip, cutting it open. She lay on the floor, whimpering.

'Get to bloody bed.'

From under the bedclothes Shirley heard the door slam as Mum came home.

'Look at the state of this place. I work all day, and come home to chaos. Where's Shirley? Why isn't the tea ready?'

'I've sent her to bed. The little cow broke all the bottles of drink, messing about with a ball, and then lied about it.'

Upstairs Shirley realised that there was no point in appealing to her mother, who never interfered when our father punished us. Most of the good hidings were at her insistence. Besides, in Mum's eyes, the boys were always more precious.

A few days later, 1946 slipped in, white and chill. It was the first January for several years that the country had not been fearful of war or at war. The world economy was precarious, but most people in England were relieved that they could go to bed and know that there was no need for black-out, and nothing would bombard them in the night.

My mother had pushed the horrors of abortion to the back of her mind, and was soon enjoying the social life that was her drug. She began to go to horse race meetings with my father, and loved the new experience. Soon gambling began to be another addiction. 'She didn't spend much,' Tony said, years later, 'But she did spend it every day, as did Dad.' Dad put his bets on through a runner at work, a man who collected the bets from the workers, and delivered them to a local bookmaker, Dobbin Holt, in his lunch hour. My mother would write out her bet before she went to work, to be taken up to the Holt's house on the outskirts of Dunstable, yet another chore for Tony or Shirley.

While Dobbin Holt was at work in a local factory, his wife ran the betting business. By the time it was my turn to make my way down her long, overgrown path, Dobbin was dead, and she lived alone. Tony said that she had always looked the same, a bent old crone, with sharp, suspicious eyes, and a white wig piled hugely and magnificently on her head. No one cheated Mrs. Holt, but she cheated others, often pretending that they had not won as much as they thought. My father checked the results meticulously, working out to the last halfpenny what he was owed. When we brought home the incorrect winnings we were promptly sent back again. I dreaded those repeat visits and stumbled through the speech I had rehearsed on the bus. 'Please Mrs. Holt, I'm sorry to trouble you, but Dad says you've made a mistake. I know how busy you are, Mrs. Holt, but Dad would be grateful if you could check the sums again. Thank you, Mrs. Holt.' I sounded ridiculous, but it was drummed into us that we must be polite to all adults and repeat the person's name when talking to them. Perhaps the old crone thought I was mocking her, for she gave me her basilisk glare. Then she disappeared into the dark depths of her cottage and spent ten minutes checking before reluctantly handing over the money. She never gave up trying to cheat him but my father was never wrong; his mathematical skills were precise.

Occasionally Mrs. Holt would be in a good mood. Perhaps she had beaten the punters, or something in her mysterious personal life had gone well. At these times she would appear at the door, with her face wreathed in smiles. She would make a comment like, 'You Darby children are so polite,' then she would hand over sixpence, or even a shilling. We learned not to tell Mum, as the money would disappear into her handbag.

My mother loved race meetings. She would take great care over her clothes, and look both beautiful and radiant as she set out, leaving Tony and Shirley to take care of the other children. Goodwood was my mother's favourite racecourse, closely followed by Epsom. That Easter they arrived there to find they couldn't gain admission unless they were members. My father turned away, ready to go home. 'But that was not Violet Darby's way,' Tony said, years later. 'She approached a man on his way in, and asked him if he would take them in as guests. Dad was mortified, but Mum laughed and chatted with the man, who said nothing would give him greater pleasure than to help such a pretty, charming lady. Once inside, he even bought them a drink.'

Life had a cautious hopefulness for the whole family as spring rolled into summer. As long as mum was happy the household had an air of precarious contentment. We all revolved around her like satellites around a planet. The only needs were hers.

With the school holidays came a sense of freedom. But the summer of 1946 could not go on for ever. We children spent long days playing in Back Field and on Dunstable Downs, ignorant of the fact that life would never seem as simple again.

With September came the return to school and nursery. It was Shirley's last year at Evelyn Road, and Roger, Roy and Jill were scattered at intervals down the school. At nursery I adored Margaret, a gentle nursery nurse, who picked me out as a special favourite. In a local newspaper photograph, taken the Christmas before, she is leaning over the table to offer a cake to another child at the nursery party. She looks kind and cheerful, predictable and reassuring.

Jill and I sit further down the table. Jill has a cake in each hand, and we both look warily at the photographer. At the back of the photograph stands Tony, waiting for the party to finish so that he can take us home.

But now, all was not well at home. Tony and Shirley remembered our mother as being particularly volatile. As the month turned into October she broke the news to our father: 'I'm pregnant.'

Shock made him illogical. 'Don't be bloody stupid, of course you're not.'

She started to cry. 'I am. There's no mistake.' She sank into the nearest chair and began to sob. 'I'm not having another abortion. I'm never going through that again. I'm going to keep this baby.'

Dad remained immobile, expressionless.

'Say something,' Mum pleaded. 'Don't stand there like a prophet of doom.'

'You're the bloody messenger with the bad news.'

She scarcely heard his mutter. 'Dabber, listen to me. I'm keeping this baby. Do you hear? It will be all right, and I have such beautiful babies.' Her tone became wheedling. 'Remember I used to say that if Hitler invaded, he'd use me for a baby machine.'

'And I used to tell you not to come out with such puerile, bloody nonsense.'

Her voice rose. 'You put me off wanting children a long time ago, with your nasty, sarcastic comments. You think you're so bloody clever with your words. When I was expecting Tony, I remember being so pleased, and you saying, "It must be the butcher's or an immaculate conception." Something beautiful you've always transformed to something sordid.'

'Lower your voice Violet. We don't want the neighbours to know our business.'

'Bugger the neighbours, and you and all.'

'For God's sake, calm down. We've got to look at this sensibly.'

'Calm down?' By now she was in a rage of fear. 'I went through an abortion last year, for you. I went to hell and back, for you. Even you were frightened when you saw the state of me afterwards.' She clenched her fists, desperate to make him understand. 'Have you ever had a knitting needle stuck up you?'

My father flinched. Then his face darkened as he stood to confront her. 'If you didn't fritter away every bloody penny that comes into this house, we wouldn't be in the state we're in now. Everything done to impress, to boast to the neighbours. And dragging me out night after night, always wanting to be the centre of attention, again trying to impress your posh friends.' He mimicked her voice, "Dabber will buy this round," as if I was bloody rolling in it.'

My mother rushed at him. He held her away from him, encasing her slim wrists in his grimy foundry hands. She spat out, her face close to his, 'If you didn't want your filthy way, I wouldn't be pregnant.'

'Never heard you say no,' he murmured, suddenly remembering that there were six silent listeners in the room, trying to blend into corners and walls. 'This is not the time or place to have this conversation. Wait until the children are in bed.'

'Don't you think they don't know what a bastard you are? The children know everything in this house.'

'More's the pity. But I'm sure you have told them that I'm all the sods unhung.' His tone was dry. 'But they'll understand when they are older.'

He glanced over at us. I looked at his expression and began to cry without knowing why. Jill joined in.

My mother ran from the room to vomit in the kitchen sink.

'Shirley, put the little ones to bed.' His voice was weary. 'And stop them crying. There's enough bloody howling going on with your mother.'

Tony opened his mouth, but didn't speak.

'They're frightened, Dad.' Shirley was surprised at her own boldness.

'We're all frightened, Shirley.'

A household where the adults have lost their way is a hellish place for children. For the next week the rows shook our home. Harsh words and sobs echoed through the house. At night we children escaped to bed. Each morning our mother struggled out of the door to work, still shaken from the vomiting which hit her as soon as she woke. In the evening, as soon as she smelled food cooking, she began to retch again. The house stank of sick and misery.

One evening Dad spoke to her in a gentle and reasonable voice. 'Violet, I think you're right not to have another abortion.'

She looked up in surprise, and wrapped her arms round his neck. 'I knew you'd see sense in the end, Dabber. We'll manage somehow.'

He pulled away from her but patted her knee. 'I've got a better idea. How would you like this baby to have all the chances in life that we can't afford to give it?'

'What do you mean?' She looked up at him, suspicious and afraid.

'We can't hope to give another child all that it needs,' he said patiently. 'And although you feel too rough to go out now of an evening, that will pass once the baby is born. Then you'll be able to enjoy yourself without worrying about a baby at home.'

My father's words were met with incredulity, then outright resistance. 'You fucking bastard.' Blinded by tears she aimed a blow at him, but he ducked and then got to his feet, waiting for her invective to come to an end.

Dad gave my mother a long level look and began again. 'What if I made sure that the baby went to a professional couple, people who could give it the very best in life? Just think, Violet, your baby could have all the things we can only dream about.'

Mum fell silent.

He held his hands out to her. 'We've six children. Far better that we raise them decently, then take on another, and all of them suffer. And in a way, you're being selfish, depriving someone who can't have children of one of yours. You know you always say how beautiful your babies are.'

She clenched her fingers in her lap and said in a voice so low he could hardly hear it, 'You bastard, you fucking bastard. I could never give up my baby.'

Dad got up and went into the back garden, to dig up vegetables.

My father knew he was racing the clock. No one outside the house had been told of the pregnancy, not even Grandma West, and he knew that none of the children would dare breathe a word to anyone. We knew 'nothing goes outside the front door.'

Soon our mother's pregnancy would be obvious. She was tall, which helped conceal her bump, but after six previous births her body would swell up readily with this seventh child. Once the neighbours started gossiping he knew she would never agree to an adoption.

Moods fluctuated. One evening Dad would reproach Mum bitterly for her profligacy, and then he would ask where they would put another baby in a house already bursting at the seams. As his mood grew ugly, he would shout, reminding Mum of the hell he went through in the months after he had raided Bagshawe's Christmas Club, wondering whether she would return to work in time to repay the money. 'And you delighted in watching me suffer, you wicked cow.'

Dad began to explain to us that families must stick together. He said a family was like a bundle of sticks. 'If one breaks away,' he explained, 'the lot disintegrate.' He felt that the only way his family could survive was by staying together. He failed to see the irony when he advocated giving one away.

The battle continued into Christmas which was subdued that year. Our father used the few days off work to have long conversations with his wife. The door of the front room was firmly shut, and the children played uneasily in the back room.

Only a quiet murmur came from behind the door. The shouting and storms had subsided. Shirley took in frequent cups of tea, and was almost unnoticed by my parents.

As he drew on a roll-up Dad narrowed his eyes through the smoke. 'Violet, I want what is right for you and the whole family. We can't afford another baby. Be grateful for the ones you've got, and look forward to a really good future.'

'How do I know that other people will be kind to my baby?'

He leaned forward. 'People who adopt babies really want them. Your baby will be loved, and have every chance in life, brought up by professional people. Just think, a doctor or a solicitor bringing up the baby, providing so much more than we ever could.'

Mum put her head in her hands and started to cry again, in resignation and acceptance.

In early January, 1947, Dr Ashton was consulted. It was one of the fiercest winters on record, and my mother wore an all-concealing flowing coat without arousing any comment. Everyone looked fatter than usual, wrapped up in numerous garments to keep warm.

Dr Ashton was sympathetic and said that he would liaise with colleagues in the town to see if any had been consulted about adopting a baby. Mum started to shake and cry. 'I don't want to know anything about who has the baby, I don't want to know anything at all.'

Dr Ashton said quietly, 'Mr. Darby, take your wife home. Come to see me on your own tomorrow. Discussing the details is too much for her.'

Once home she wept all evening. When the tears finally stopped she turned to our father and said, 'The only way I can go through with this is never to see the baby. If I do, I know that I'll never give it up.'

My father leaned towards her and his voice was gentle. 'You have my word about that. In a few months this will all be over, and you'll have forgotten all about it. You'll even forget you were ever pregnant.'

He sat thinking, and then said, 'Violet, we've never been on holiday. The baby will be born in May. When the kids break up from school we'll go away to the seaside: just keep your mind fixed on that.'

Our mother gave up work a short time later. She was afraid that her colleagues would guess she was pregnant. She scarcely left the house, and the neighbours were told that she was having a few months off to spend more time with her children. Dr Ashton visited her at home, usually after dark.

Today, a file on a prospective adoption would be dense, but the 1947 file was a mere few, badly typed sheets. The investigator is asked:

What are your impressions of a) the petitioners and b) their home and surroundings?

and the response states coldly:
- *a) Sound reliable people in every respect.*
- *b) A very nice home, tastefully furnished and very clean and tidy with a homely atmosphere. Child is assured of every care and comfort.*

The authorities were not altogether satisfied with the situation. The closest anyone came to questioning my parents' reasons for having their seventh child adopted was the School Welfare and Enquiry Officer. He wrote:

In my report, it will be noted that the reason given for adoption, given by the natural parents of the child, is that it would be impossible for them to bring the child up suitably, although the wages of Mr. Darby are £9.6s weekly, plus £1.5s family allowance. This, I regret to say, is the only information I can obtain upon this point.

My mother knew nothing of all these negotiations. Neither did she know that our father had withheld the information that her wages had practically equalled his. As far as the authorities were concerned she stayed at home to look after her children as most mothers did. The Court decided to take the investigations no further, and gave leave for the adoption proceedings.

Ironically, Dad was vindicated in his accusations about the way his wife spent money. Even the officer concerned could not understand why they could not afford this child, but the officer was not informed about the drinking, socialising and gambling, and the clothes Mum just had to have.

In May, she went into The Chase Nursing Home to give birth. There was no way she could have this child at home without seeing the baby, and also the neighbours finding out. In later rows with Dad she claimed she was not treated well at The Chase, that she was left alone in the final stages of labour until the very last minute, and that she fell off the bed in her agony. Did the nurses disapprove? Or did Mum fear that they disapproved?

My father kept his word and she never saw her baby. The seventh Darby child, and fourth daughter was taken straight from the room, leaving Mum bereft. The baby girl was a week- old before she went to her adoptive parents. Where she was during her first week of life is not recorded. Did she go to a foster mother? I think it more probable that she was kept at The Chase.

My mother stayed for the minimum length of time possible in The Chase. Dad took her home and sent Shirley to Chorleys, the shop on the corner, for some biscuits for Mum to eat with a cup of tea. At home there had been no mention of a baby for a long time, and Shirley was unaware that one had been born. Her parents had said nothing. Dad had said Mum was in hospital to cure her of all the sickness she had been suffering. Tony had realised the true state of affairs, but had been warned by his father to say nothing at all to the rest of us.

Shirley hurried into the shop and encountered the usual group of neighbours, gathered for a chat as they did their shopping. 'Hello, Shirley,' said one cheerfully. 'Did we see your mother coming home a little while ago?'

'Yes, she's better now.'

'That's good, have you got a little brother or sister?'

Not knowing what to say, Shirley guessed, 'A brother.'

'That's nice, What's his name?'

Shirley felt anxious. 'I don't know,' and clutching the biscuits she ran home.

When Shirley told her parents about the incident, both were angry. Her father snapped, 'You stupid little cow.

You should have said they were wrong, that Mum hadn't had a baby.'

A confused Shirley ran from the room, down the garden, and into Back Field. The neighbourhood children were playing a game of tag. 'Come and play, Shirley, we need some more people.'

Shirley joined in, running round like a dervish, laughing hysterically.

Two days after the baby's birth Dad was summoned once more to see Dr Ashton.

'A successful outcome, Mr. Darby. The baby girl is doing well. The Chase Nursing Home will keep her for a few more days and then she will go to her new home. There is much excited anticipation there.'

'That's good.' Dad fumbled for words.

'Yes, and Mrs. Darby is recovering well. I called into your home to see her this morning; she's very tearful but that is to be expected. Now...registering the birth.'

'I'm taking a couple of hours off work next Thursday to register the baby, Doctor. Violet usually does it, but she refuses point blank this time. Anyway, while she's refusing to know whether the baby is a boy or a girl, it will be impossible.'

'Indeed. Mr. Darby, the new parents want you to register the little girl as 'Judy.'

Dad laughed, half in shock. 'I've already got a child called Judy.'

'I know you have, but...this one won't be yours in a few months. She'll belong to someone else.'

'Don't they know that there is a sister who has that name?'

'They know nothing about the siblings except that they are healthy and intelligent. They didn't want or need to know anything else. They long for this child as much as you long to get rid of it.'

Dad winced, and silence fell for a few moments as the two men sat thinking.

'Judy is the only name I chose,' Dad said. 'Violet was taken off to hospital the night she was born, and she told Shirley that she could choose the name. Shirley wanted some sort of nonsense like Sally Ann...'

'A lovely name,' interposed Dr Ashton.

'Maybe, anyway I didn't think so at the time, so I told her it had to be something sensible like Judith.'

'Seems as if a lot of thought went into it.'

'You try coping with a household of small children, a new baby and a wife who's dying; see how much thought you'd give it.'

Dr Ashton hastened to calm Dad. 'I fully understand. All I'm saying is that it can't matter too much to you, and even if it does the two children won't be under the same roof. There'll be no confusion. Mrs. Darby is unaware that she has a daughter, so where's the problem? The baby will ultimately receive that name anyway.'

'Perhaps you're right.' Dad paused and thought. 'What the hell does it matter?'

On June 4th, 1947, a second Darby child was registered with the name of Judy.

In the weeks following the birth, my mother came close to breaking point. My father's holiday materialised, but they only took four children with them. Jill was sent to Chesham again, to stay with kind Auntie Lily and Uncle Ted.

I was left with Mrs. Coombes who lived next door, the opposite side from the doubtful Keithy Lewis.

On the morning the family left to go to Folkestone it was obvious something was happening as my mother and Shirley packed clothes and threw out perishable food. Dad left first with Tony, Shirley, Roger and Roy, as they had agreed to wait down the road. Then Mum took me next door to Mrs. Coombes. 'I'm just going shopping, Judy,' she said, her tone bright. 'You stay with Mrs. Coombes, and play with Monty, her dog.'

I began to cry. 'I want to come with you. I want Shirley.'

'Don't be silly, I'm just going shopping, to Luton. I'll be back soon,' and with a wave and smile, she disappeared down the road. I stood at the gate, which was firmly closed, and grasped the wooden spokes, with tears streaming down my face. I didn't know where she was going, but I knew it wasn't shopping, and I was certain she would never come back.

In Tony's words, the Folkestone holiday was an unmitigated disaster. The boarding house, under railway arches, was dirty, and the food was unpalatable. Mum was disappointed, and made her feelings clear. The weather was beautiful, and Roger became red and raw from the sun. He cried miserably at night until threatened with a good hiding.

Folkestone, 1947

A photograph shows our mother bulging slightly out of her dress, as she had still to regain her figure after the birth. The four children, Tony, Shirley, Roger and Roy, stand scrubbed and obedient, but no one looks as if they are enjoying themselves. Roy is wearing a little cotton shirt and shorts set that is too tight for him, and Shirley remembers him becoming very sore.

As the weeks passed bringing the adoption hearing nearer, my mother slept little. She wondered what her child looked like. And, knowing no details, she could only imagine her baby's home. She believed that her baby had gone to the home of a solicitor, and my father did nothing to make her think differently, so she did not know that the baby had been taken to a working class couple less than two miles away, in the same small town.

'She's still mine,' she told Dad, 'right up until the final papers are signed.'

My mother was referring to the hearing. She had already signed the papers, but had no idea what they contained as she refused to read them.

Then came the night when she cried to have her baby returned to her. The animal howls spread through the house, and we children woke in fear as we heard her despair.

My father told her that it was too late. No court would remove a baby from its new parents after three months had elapsed. This was never to be put to the test. Either my mother believed him, or she couldn't face the fight.

The day arrived when her baby was legally made the child of another family.

Dad sighed with relief. The months of hell were now over.

Private adoptions are no longer legal in this country, and so the practice of GPs placing children locally cannot happen. The casual investigation of family background is also a fact of the past, but no parent is forced to keep a child.

Chapter 6: Felpham

The holiday in Folkestone was a mistake. If my father believed he could take his wife's mind off her grief, he was wrong. A change of environment proved to be only a temporary distraction.

Roger's miserable holiday was compounded by the fact that he did not even wish to be there. The day the family set off for Folkestone he was discharged from hospital, after spending six weeks in an isolation ward with scarlet fever. He had loved his time in hospital, with its regular meals in a calm atmosphere, and playing with the other children in the ward. He had learned that there was another world of friendly predictability to which he wanted to cling, and he travelled to Folkestone in tears.

In August 1947, back from holiday, with Jill home from Chesham, and me retrieved from next door, the family was once more complete. Or so it seemed. But over the household hung a dark question mark. The atmosphere was charged and uneasy. Mum no longer cried, or at least we no longer heard her, but her temper was increasingly uncertain, and she threw herself once more into a manic social round. As she got ready in the evenings she was febrile, laughing, hugging and kissing all of us before we went to sleep. When she came home late, both Shirley and Tony made sure they had joined the younger ones in bed, for there was no knowing her mood. Sometimes her laugh rang through the house, and she would go into the bedrooms, to kiss sleeping children, and at other times we would hear her shout and swear, and there were angry exchanges between her and my father.

My mother was exhausted. She had given up her previous job halfway through her pregnancy, before her condition became noticeable. Now she had started working again, in a cigarette factory. The work was unskilled and her pay was much lower than before. All day she stood packing cigarettes, and her feet hurt to such an extent that she bought a pair of short fur boots, two sizes too big, and padded them out with socks. She also took advantage of their size to slip cigarettes inside to take home for my father. The job's one consolation was the company, for the women she worked with were friendly, although she considered herself superior to them. But no one at work knew her secret, and she felt that she could relax.

My mother's exhaustion seemed a spur to her socialising; she found it necessary to fill every hour of the day. Once more she went out with her smart friends, in particular the Summerfields. Henry Summerfield was already a borderline alcoholic. But at the time he ran a thriving building business in the town, and could scarcely keep pace with the post-war building boom.

Shirley was due to attend grammar school in September, where Valerie Summerfield was already in her fourth year.

'Shirley can have Valerie's outgrown uniform,' said Mrs. Summerfield. 'It's ridiculous forking out for new clothes when you can have them for free.'

Our mother was delighted. Unfortunately for Shirley, even Valerie's first year cast-offs were much too big, and she looked like a malnourished orphan. What was worse, the uniform had changed in the intervening years, and Shirley was the only first year who wore the old-style uniform. She felt resigned. She knew in advance that absence would be a problem, that she would not have the ingredients for cookery lessons, that often she would be without dinner money, that she would be sneered at for being different. Stoicism sat on her shoulder like a guardian angel, protecting her from despair.

Mum had been fearful of what the neighbours might say to her after she returned from the nursing home, and Shirley's encounter in the local shop had revealed that they knew she had given birth. For months she ventured out only to work, or in the evenings with Dad. She no longer had chats in Chorley's corner shop, and the only neighbours she spoke to were her friends Mabel Coombes, next door, and Daisy Brown a few doors down. Daisy and Ezra Brown had lived next door when my parents lived up the hill, and it was Daisy who had stayed with our mother after the birth of Shirley, as our father frantically raced for Dr Ashton. Both Mabel and Daisy were kind, discreet women, who made no comment to Mum, although it was inevitable that they *knew*.

Gradually, my mother became bolder, and one day actually stood chatting at the garden gate to a woman who lived further down the road. Jill was standing beside her mother.

'Everyone says how polite your children are,' said the woman, her eyes travelling over Jill and taking in every detail.

Our mother smiled. 'Dabber and I lay down strict rules for the children. We believe there is nothing worse than a badly behaved child.'

'I expect you need to be strict with so many children.'

Mum nodded uncertainly.

'And wasn't there another baby, too?'

My mother burst into tears. 'I don't know what you're talking about. Of course there wasn't another baby. Jill, come on, we're going indoors.'

My mother rushed down the garden path, pushing Jill ahead of her. The little girl stumbled, and Mum grabbed her roughly by the arm, hurrying her along. When my father came home that night he was met by a tearful wife.

'Dabber, we can't stay here, we can't. All the neighbours are talking about my baby. They must all be laughing and whispering behind my back. I can't bear it. We've got to move.'

'Let me get through the door before you start.' Dad's voice was weary. 'And why are you bothered about what bloody neighbours say?'

She slammed his dinner down in front of him, tears replaced by anger. 'It's all right for you. You don't have to face the looks and whispers. I live in dread of them making comments to me, and what do I say when some are rude enough to ask me questions?'

My father looked irritated. 'You tell them to bugger off, that's what you do. I'd like to see any of them try it with me.'

My mother sighed. 'They wouldn't. You know they wouldn't. Everyone respects you, and thinks you're really clever because of your lectures to the police in the war. If they need to write a difficult official letter they come to you, if they want anything explained they come to you. Daisy Brown says you're a walking encyclopaedia. She also says that everyone is really impressed by the way you're negotiating with the landlord for us to buy these houses.'

My father snorted. 'That doesn't take much intelligence. He wants to sell as many of this row of houses as possible, but won't do so unless he gets a majority wanting to buy. Luckily he's selling at such a reasonable price that most of the neighbours can afford to buy and get a mortgage.'

My mother beckoned to Shirley to come and clear the plates, and said, 'Well the neighbours all think you're wonderful, whatever they think of me.' Then she brightened up. We're meeting the Summerfields tonight. I'm looking forward to that, anyway.'

It was Dad's turn to sigh. 'Another bloody expensive evening.'

That evening my parents sat in a quaint rural pub a few miles out of Dunstable. The Summerfields came through the door, and while Phyllis Summerfield sat down next to my mother, her husband took my father to one side. 'I've got a proposition for you, Aubrey.'

Dad looked at him warily. 'And what might that be?'

'Well, you're just about to buy your house at a bargain price. But those houses in Luton Road were never meant to house a family with six children. Why don't you send Vi and the children to the coast for a year while I build you a lovely house at the foot of Dunstable Downs? I've just acquired a nice piece of land there and I'm putting in for planning permission.'

Dad smiled. 'Come off it Henry. I could never afford your fancy prices.'

Henry Summerfield slapped him on the back and roared with laughter. 'I didn't make my money in house building by robbing people. I'm offering you a good deal. When you sell the Luton Road house you'll have a substantial deposit.' He leaned forward confidentially. 'The wife thinks Vi is looking peaky. A year by the sea will work wonders for her health. You can stay with your mother or hers, and join the family at weekends.'

My father looked at his friend. How much did he know or guess? Illness had been used as the reason for the months they had stayed away from people, when my mother had feared that her condition was all too obvious. Mrs. Summerfield had sharp eyes and would have realised immediately. Had she put two and two together and guessed the truth? She would not comment as she was too discreet for that, but it left my father with an uncomfortable feeling.

Nothing more was said that evening, but on the way home my mother wanted to know about the whispered conversation. My father was laconic. 'He wants to build us a big house the other side of Dunstable. Bloody nonsense.'

Mum clapped her hands. 'It's not nonsense. A big house, just think of it.' Then another thought struck her. 'Oh Dabber, I could get away from the neighbours and their gossip. We could make a fresh start.'

My father was far from keen, but since the adoption Mum had increasingly got her own way. It was as if the massive fight he had put up, and the sustained arguments, had taken the will to win out of him. Perhaps he felt guilty when he reflected how she had suffered. Whatever the reason, within a few days he had agreed to sell the house and move the family down to Sussex for a year. A small house would be rented in Felpham Village, near Bognor, and his wife and children would live there while he stayed with Grandma West and continued working at Bagshawe's. He would join us at weekends.

But first of all 322 Luton Road must be made fit to sell. My father paid for a decorator to paint and wallpaper the house from top to bottom. He considered that this would push up the value of the house. The house looked smart and the children were threatened with good hidings if it wasn't kept that way. The pristine white walls in the boys' bedroom fascinated ten-year-old Roger, and he found some creosote in the garden shed. With an enormous brush kept for the purpose of treating the garden fence, he painted a picture of a man peeing on a pot right in the middle of the wall. When Tony saw the crude drawing he was horrified. 'The old man will murder you when he sees that,' he said.

Roger attempted bravado. 'I thought it would make a nice picture for the wall. It looked too plain.'

'You're raving mad. He'll kill you.'

As the time approached for his father's return from work Roger disappeared, and crept home late that night. Dad was by the back door, his fury fuelled by the waiting. Roger's cries rang through the house as, with tongue between his teeth, eyes afire, Dad thrashed him.

The creosote proved stronger than any coat of paint, and every time a viewing was booked for the house Dad would slap on a covering layer of whiteness. Within a few days the shape of the man and his pot would make an eerie appearance, and cursing, Dad would reach for the paint and brush once again. Roger took care to keep out of sight at those times. The day we moved out the man was making yet another appearance.

By the time of our move to Felpham I had been at Evelyn Road School for a year, where I very happy. Miss Greenwood's favour rested on the bright, and she could be cruel to those who struggled. With five brothers and sisters ahead of me who had all done well, I was welcome in the school and I loved its order, the colourful classroom and the abundance of books. The teaching was excellent, the school dinners delicious. I was a quiet, withdrawn child, happy in a corner with a book. I loved chanting tables each morning as the mindless activity had a comforting ritual about it. At Evelyn Road all was predictable, and I revelled in the narrow confines which fitted as snugly as a strait jacket.

At Dunstable Grammar School the headmaster heard the news of Tony's impending departure to Sussex with some dismay. He asked my father and Tony to come to see him.

'Mr. Darby, Dunstable School would be extremely sorry to lose Tony at this stage. He has two years to go before Higher School Certificate and university entrance.'

My father shifted uncomfortably. 'I realise that, but family circumstances make it necessary. He can attend Chichester High School for his lower sixth year.'

The headmaster looked first at Dad and then at Tony. He steepled his fingers and then spoke very slowly and deliberately. 'I have been in touch with Chichester School. The syllabus for Tony's subjects is different from ours as they use a different examination board. He will be at a considerable disadvantage when he returns to us.'

My father looked miserable. 'I'm sorry about that, but there is nothing I can do.'

Silence fell and then the headmaster cleared his throat. 'Before the Education Act we were a public school. You know that of course, as Tony was a pupil here for a year before the Act, winning one of our prestigious scholarships.'

My father wondered where all this was leading, but sensed it wasn't small talk and was also likely to cause him problems.

The Head continued, 'We still have a small boarding house. I have spoken to the governors and we would be prepared to keep Tony as a boarder for this coming year.'

'I'm sorry Headmaster, but I couldn't possibly afford to pay that sort of money.'

'There would be no charge Mr. Darby. We find Tony a valuable pupil, both in the classroom and on the sports field. He is also a natural leader. We would consider it a privilege to keep him.'

My father searched for words which would not come. His eyes met Tony's and he winced at the hope he saw there, knowing he was about to destroy it. 'But I need Tony to be with his mother in Felpham while I am not there. She cannot manage without him.'

A few weeks later, the removal van moved slowly away from 322 Luton Road. Inside was everything our family possessed, plus the dog, cat and all the children. The car had been sold and our parents went by train. The removal men grumbled about their extra cargo even though Dad had tipped them generously. Mercifully I cannot recall that journey.

Nearly four hours later the van drew up outside a row of small cottages in Felpham. My first impressions were the assault of sharp salty air, the whirling, circling, screeching seagulls and the heavy dragging sound of the sea retreating over the pebbly shore. I was overwhelmed by the difference in the atmosphere.

'Breathe in the ozone,' said my father. 'It's good for the lungs.'

The house was smaller than the one in Luton Road. There was no front garden, and a minute back one which was accessed by a narrow side alley. The bathroom led off the tiny kitchen and there were two cramped reception rooms. Upstairs three bedrooms grouped round a small square landing. This was to be our home for the next ten months.

The beach was two hundred yards away at the bottom of our road, a cul-de-sac. A short alley way cut through the sea front buildings to take us straight down to the shingle, sand and sea. Once the winter nights set in I could hear the violence of the waves as they lashed the fragile defences, and clung closer to Jill and Shirley in bed.

Tony, Shirley and Roger all attended the single sex grammar schools in nearby Chichester. It was Roger's first year in secondary education as he had left Evelyn Road that summer. Tony never protested about his move from Dunstable Grammar and his missed opportunities, but settled down at Chichester. Shirley joined the third year of the sister school in the full knowledge that she would spend more time at home than at school.

Roy, Jill and I went to the village school in Felpham. It was very different from Evelyn Road, which was a modern building ahead of its time. Felpham School was built in 1887, very much a Victorian structure. A plaque, still on the original building, now converted to private homes, records:

These schools were dedicated to the glory of God and the religious education of the little ones of Christ's flock on the first day of February 1887.

By 1949 the school had long outgrown its building, and plans had been drawn in 1946 for a new school, although it was 1957 before it was finally opened. In the meantime the village school limped on, with its lavatories across the other side of the tiny playground. If it rained, the pupils got soaked, running across to the smelly hut clutching the sheet of rough paper rationed for such visits. Asking for a sheet of paper could be embarrassing, but the sub standard paper itself did not worry us as most of the pupils used newspaper at home.

There was no grass to play on in the macadamised school playground, ironic in a village surrounded by fields, the River Rife and the beach. Roger became friendly with a local fisherman called Stan, and a stout lad called Pud. The three spent hours out in Stan's fishing boat.

Once, when Pud knocked, I opened the door and called out, 'Roger, Pudding is at the door.' Everyone laughed. I had thought Pud was a diminutive and that it was impolite to use it.

I cannot remember making any friends at the school, although Jill and Roy quickly became popular. But they had no affection for the school either. It was useless trying to join their groups of friends as age groups in schools rarely mix. I stood alone in the playground one day, feeling isolated and vulnerable. Seeing Roy a few yards away kicking a ball effortlessly to a new friend, I walked over to him. In time honoured fashion he told me to 'run away and play shops.' This was the brother who spent many painstaking hours teaching me to play cricket, whist and monopoly. It didn't matter about sibling friendship at home, in school you must stay with your peers.

The head teacher scared me although he rarely came to my classroom. The school was one class entry for children from five to eleven years, just like Evelyn Road. At the time I was approaching my sixth birthday. My class had a young woman teacher who was usually pleasant to me, but I found it hard to like her as I was never quite sure what she expected. However, the classroom was regimented and we were expected to be able to work in a formal way. Arithmetic lessons were torture. We all had different cards to work from, setting out sums in our arithmetic books. Nowadays such diversity would be termed differentiation, but that is not what was happening in that classroom at that time. You were given any card to work from, irrespective of ability. On my first day I was given a card of addition sums where the units totalled more than nine. We called this carrying, and I had not the faintest idea where to begin. The thorough grounding at Evelyn Road had ensured that although I knew my tables inside out and could count backwards and forwards to one hundred in all sorts of convoluted ways, I could not do carrying sums. I doubt that any others in the class could either. There was no practical apparatus, no counters, no cubes.

For some reason it did not occur to the teacher to check whether I could do the sums by rote, let alone understand the concept involved. Frightened and dumbstruck, I sat at the back of the classroom struggling to do the first sum. I realised that I could not have two numbers in the units column and so rubbed anxiously at the two numbers jostling there. My finger was grubby and I made a hideous mess. I rubbed harder in an effort to erase the numbers and the filthy black marks. Inevitably a big hole appeared in the page surrounded by finger marks.

The teacher's method of correcting work was to sit at her desk and call out children one by one with their books. There were about forty children in the class, and as the arithmetic lesson was not very long it took her some time to work round everyone. For days I sat there in terror until I was called out to her desk.

The teacher's rebuke was mild. I was not asked what I didn't understand, but given an easier card with the reproving words, 'Judy, I'm disappointed in you. I thought you could do better than that.' She never explained whether she meant my filthy book, my lack of ability, or both. I was happy to be out of an intolerable situation. But the experience coloured my brief time there. I was always fearful of work I couldn't do, which set up a dread of going to school

I treasured reading. The enjoyment was always there, but when life became difficult, reality could be exchanged for fantasy. With reading came the ability to write. But I soon discovered little was expected in my class at the village school. One Monday morning we were asked to write about the weekend. Our exercise books were the equivalent of what is now A5, cut in half, so a page was very small. We were asked to draw a picture under our writing. No further help or instructions were given, but I was happy. I had plenty to write about my father coming home at the weekends, and my mother being unhappy on Sunday night, and what we all did during the two days. I covered page after page of the tiny book with my large round printing. I ran out of time and was unable to draw a picture. Then we were sent out to play, and when we came back in the children wandered round looking at each other's work. When they saw mine they told me that I would be in big trouble because you weren't meant to use up so much paper. You were meant to write a sentence and draw a picture on one page.

At first I didn't believe them, for I couldn't imagine plump, comfortable Miss Barton back at Evelyn Road being cross if I had written a lot. I knew she would have been pleased and sent me to show Miss Greenwood. But my classmates were right although they were in trouble too. The teacher expressed disapproval of the fact that most of them had written, 'At the weekend I swing on my swing,' duly illustrated. She said that she would never again let them talk while writing, because the idea must have travelled round the classroom.

Then she turned her attention to me. I had written far too much and wasted paper. There was no need to write more than a sentence or perhaps two. Where, also, was my picture? I admitted that I had run out of time and she was triumphant, saying that I had proved her point. All my pleasure in my writing evaporated.

Even as a child I recognised that this was very different from the arithmetic situation. I had confidence in my reading and writing abilities, my favourite hobbies. I often spent my occasional Saturday threepence on an exercise book bought from the village shop. Even as I sat weeping at the teacher's rebuke, I knew that I must conform and would no longer find enjoyment in the work; I lived in terror of stepping outside boundaries.

I also remember the village school for its appalling dinners. The potatoes were black and lumpy, the frogspawn (tapioca) was foul. Semolina came out in lumpy slices, and meat consisted largely of gristle. But the horrible concoction which gave me nightmares, and kept me awake at night fearing it would be on the next day's menu, was salad cream. Salad days were black days. Carrying our plates we moved slowly along the line as the dinner ladies apportioned a slice of cold, fatty meat, a dollop of virtually inedible potato, lettuce leaves that had been plucked from the ground months ago, and half a decaying tomato. These were submerged in salad cream.

I felt sick. Even the sight of the salad cream jug would make my stomach heave. I managed to whisper that I would rather not have salad cream, answered sometimes with, 'What nonsense!' Mostly I was ignored. After the meal I would go outside and be violently sick.

One night I lay sobbing in bed at the prospect of the torture. Jill became alarmed and called for Shirley, who told my parents that I would need a letter to stop the school making me eat it. My father said he would write it, but as we all sat cramped round the table eating Sunday dinner he suddenly pointed his knife at me, chewing furiously. 'Are you sure you're not making this up?' I felt his eyes slicing through me, and my own filled with tears.

'Quite the little actress,' said my mother.

Shirley jumped to my rescue. 'The salad cream makes her sick. She's not even six yet, it's not fair.'

My father gave me an icy, level look. I shivered, but he appeared satisfied and returned to his dinner. But at intervals he would glance at me, straight across the table, and suddenly it was all too much and I began to sob hysterically.

'For God's sake, get out of the room,' said Dad, and as I went I saw Roger grab my dinner.

After dinner Dad wrote the letter, and I felt happy until Roy said, 'They won't be able to read Dad's handwriting. Only Mum can.'

I turned in panic to Shirley who promised to copy it out in her neat script after Dad had left to make his Sunday night journey back to Dunstable. She had to guess at some of the words but it was close enough to what he had written.

I went to school the next morning, clutching the letter, folded over without an envelope. The feeling of relief was tremendous and I looked forward to school dinner time.

Christmas Day was a happy day in our home. A whole day without rows of any description. We always received presents and had a big dinner which my father usually cooked with Shirley's help. He always made a suet pudding, parcelled up in an old cloth like a figure eight, which we ate with the chicken and vegetables. We felt satisfied and content. That year in Felpham My father arrived home on Christmas Eve afternoon with his seasonal bonus, and my mother and Shirley hurried out to buy food and presents.

But Christmas was a lull in an anxious year. The time in Felpham was a difficult one. Mum found it difficult to cope with any child stepping out of line without the threat of our father coming home at the end of each day, and increasingly relied on Tony and Shirley, aged sixteen and fourteen, to run the home and organise the younger children. There was nothing new in that, but the eldest two also had to adjust to the new environment and new schools.

Hardly had our father entered the house on a Friday evening when Mum would reel off a catalogue of the younger ones' wrongdoings. He would be tired after a week in the foundry, and tense from the journey from Luton to Bognor Regis on a platform ticket, always alert, watching for an inspector.

'Those journeys were hell,' he told me in later years.

Naively I asked, 'Then why didn't you buy a proper ticket?' not understanding the poverty of that time: the payment for board to Grandma West, the rent for the Felpham house, the money Mum spent when he wasn't around to keep an eye on her, and the indisputable fact that her earnings at Luton Road had made all the difference. She had no job in Felpham.

So his return to the family on a Friday night was not always happy. Sometimes he would say, 'For God's sake let me get through the door before you start,' but more often than not he would give good hidings to a child or two so that fear and obedience settled over the house like some malignant spirit.

One Friday he arrived home exhausted, to be greeted with a list of children who deserved good hidings. It was inevitable that Roger and Roy pushed their luck once their father's heavy hand was one hundred miles away. But this evening his reaction was unexpected, and we were amazed to hear him say, 'I'm not coming home every Friday to beat seven bells out of my children. Do you want them to end up terrified of me? I want to be more to them that that. Learn to control them your bloody self.'

There was a very strong reason for anxiety. Mum had intended looking for work in Felpham, but in late September, a bare three weeks after our move, she discovered she was pregnant yet again.

My father was unnaturally quiet at this revelation. For a few weeks he maintained this reticence and seemed relieved to escape back to Bedfordshire and work on a Sunday night. He never liked to think deeply about anything he found painful. However, he had weathered Mum's anguish after parting with her baby with apparent stoicism. He had convinced her that it was for the best, that it was a rational and pragmatic decision. Now he was faced with a fresh dilemma, and the financial implications, which were grim.

In less than a year the family would be returning to Dunstable, to a newly-built house practically twice the size of 322 Luton Road. To complete the house he would need to have garden walls built and gates installed. The rates would be doubled, the upkeep very expensive. With a new baby my mother would not be able to work for a while, and there were already signs that her health was permanently failing.

The answer was to continue to stay on for a while in Felpham and sell the new house without ever living in it. Then buy a smaller house in Dunstable and cut his losses. He considered giving up the new house, and starting afresh in Sussex because Tony remembered him going for a managerial role at a firm in Chichester, a few miles from Felpham. The money would have been more than he was earning, and he was interviewed and offered the job. After a sleepless night he turned the offer down as he felt he would not know how to conduct himself in meetings. With his inexperience of such matters he felt that the discussions would be erudite and above his head, rather than the 90% hot air that is often spoken in meetings. It was very sad as Dad's formidable brain would have brought a freshness and lack of nonsense to the job. The managing director thought that he was the man he wanted and was disappointed at his decision.

Years later my father told me that he wished he'd put down roots in Felpham, his only spoken regret. The family was about to move back to Dunstable a few months later, to a house which he could not afford, and his wife was pregnant with an eighth child. This time he made no attempt to persuade her to have the baby adopted. By now it was painfully clear what the loss of her previous baby had done to her emotionally. However, her health was affected almost from the start, and her soaring blood pressure meant she spent part of each day in bed. Shirley's attendance at her new school became spasmodic. She and Tony did their best to keep things running smoothly, but the atmosphere at the weekends was heavy and apprehensive.

Although my father considered the alternative of a cheaper house in Dunstable he did not voice it. My mother's reaction would have been more than he could cope with, and he had no wish to destroy her childlike excitement over the new, smart house, and no energy left for a fight or even for long, reasoned discussions. Worn and tired, he was a different man from three years previously, with much of the spirit knocked out of him.

At weekends and school holidays in Felpham, the four younger children were expected to be outdoors for most of the day. Roger and Roy would disappear after breakfast, and Jill and I would reluctantly make our way to the beach. Often we were cold and miserable, and would go back home and plead to be allowed in.

'Go away,' called our mother, without opening the door. 'You'll be complaining that you haven't got a beach to play on when we move back to Dunstable. You're lucky children; now go and play on the beach. Keep away from the sea. I don't want you drowning yourselves.'

There were times when we hated the sea as we shivered in shrill breezes, huddled close to keep warm. When the weather turned mild we would stand and watch the day trippers buying ice-cream, in frank envy.

'We were urchins,' Jill said recently, 'nothing but urchins.' And we were, often hungry, ill-clad, and wearing shoes with the soles coming off as sand clung to our toes.

One Friday night in March my father arrived home looking old and defeated. His eyes were dull and heavy. When our mother, now heavily pregnant and bored with bed rest, began on her usual litany, he interrupted her harshly. 'Violet, I have some sad news.'

'It can't be any more sad than what I have to put up with, stuck here in this shoe-box, with kids who don't do as they're told.'

For a moment Dad's eyes darted angrily, but the spark died, and when he spoke his voice was expressionless. 'My mother died earlier this week. There was no way to let you know.'

My mother looked abashed for a moment, then she rallied. 'Well she's been going downhill for some time. It was probably a merciful release. And eighty-four is a good age.'

My father sat down heavily on a chair and examined his filthy, foundry finger nails as if he had never seen them before. 'Yes, she was swollen with dropsy. It took four men to lift her body off the bed after she died.' His voice broke. 'Poor Ma. She was a good woman.'

My mother moved impatiently. 'Well her suffering is over now. When's the funeral?

For a long moment my father said nothing. Then he looked straight at his wife. 'Hettie told me she was arranging it for one day next week, but she's had it brought forward to tomorrow.'

We all became conscious of my mother's breathing. I grabbed hold of Jill who was already backing into a corner.

'You needn't think you're going back tomorrow leaving me to cope alone with everything here for the weekend, in my condition.' Noisy and uncontrolled she began to cry.

'It's my mother. I've got to go. I want to go.'

Mum picked up an ashtray. It flew past Dad's ear and shattered against the wall. I stuffed my already well-chewed cuff into my mouth.

Eyes glittering, the tears suddenly dried, her voice became like acid, cold and biting. 'You can go to the funeral when Hettie shares out some of your mother's linen and other possessions. We've as much right to them as Hettie, any day of the week.'

My father's face paled.

'It's my mother,' he repeated, as if he could not believe what he was hearing. 'My mother, it's her funeral.'

'And I'm telling you to stand up to Hettie and demand what is your right. Are you a man or a mouse?' She spat the words at him, her contempt tangible. 'And if you think you're leaving me to cope here while you go back to Luton tomorrow you've got another fucking thought coming.'

Before our eyes our father crumpled, and tears began to slide down his face. Shirley gave a little cry, and ran out of the door, down to the beach, where she walked and walked, unable to get the sight of her father's suffering out of her mind.

When she finally returned to the house all was quiet. Tony was in the kitchen, grim-faced, washing up. Mum had gone back to bed, and the rest of us were playing Monopoly in a corner of the room as if trying to separate ourselves from the scene which had been played out.

'Where's Dad?'

'Upstairs with Mum. She's crying and having palpitations and he's trying to calm her down.'

'In other words she's won?'

Tony nodded. 'Oh yes. He won't be going to any funeral.'

As the summer of 1950 warmed the sand and shingle, the beach became a more welcome place. Roger decided I should learn to swim. It was a blustery day when he led me over the shingle to the grey waves tipped with what I thought was washing powder. Roger allowed me to believe that. 'Keep your mouth shut Jude, as the soap will make you sick.'

I was commanded to climb on his back and assured that he would swim out a little way and then back to shore, so that I would get the feel of the water and acclimatise to the temperature. Always trusting, I believed him. That was stupid: only the week before he had knocked my two front teeth out teaching me to field at cricket. He consoled me by telling me that all the best cricketers caught the ball in their mouths, but his quick thinking did not prevent him receiving one of his frequent good hidings.

But that morning I climbed on his back. The water struck harsh, bitter and biting. I started to scream. 'I want to go home; I'm scared.'

Roger ignored me. At twelve he was lean and muscular, and he swam boldly towards the horizon. Then, without warning, he flicked me off his back, 'Swim, Jude, swim.'

Terrified, I tried to cling to him, but he swam away. I went under again and again. Spluttering, I swallowed sea water, vomited, went under once more, and was barely conscious of a strong grip, stronger than Roger's, grabbing my pigtails and towing me back to shore. Tony had seen everything as he came through the alley from our road, and raced to the rescue.

For his attempts to help me swim Roger added another good hiding to his tally. I finally overcame my fear of water at fifteen when I learned to swim.

Meanwhile school was still a place of uncertainty where I dreaded each day. I dimly realised that we were not staying in Felpham for ever, and I dreamed of a time when I would return to Evelyn Road School where I had been so happy.

One evening Shirley boiled a kettle to wash Jill and me in the kitchen. As she took the kettle off the gas Jill and I started to fool around and nudge each other. I stumbled into Shirley and the water scalded my arm. Screaming with pain I ran up and down the hall. Later the arm came up in enormous blisters and the doctor cut them, as was the practice then. Evil looking liquid poured out into a bowl. A doctor at the hospital in Chichester advised that I should be kept at home to avoid the arm becoming knocked or infected, and as we returned to Dunstable shortly after that, I never saw the inside of Felpham Village School again.

On Roy and Jill's last day the headmaster bade them a courteous farewell and asked them to say goodbye to me. There was no message from my class teacher and I did not wish for one. I was going home, back to Dunstable and Evelyn Road. Roy and Jill would also return to Evelyn Road.

Roger would have to start a second grammar school after completing only a year at Chichester. Shirley, aged fifteen would leave school to find a job. Tony would also leave school altogether. The Headmaster of Dunstable

Grammar had been correct in his assertion that the sixth form syllabus would be different at Chichester. So, stranded in the middle of a two-year course, Tony agreed with Dad that he should leave school to work in a bank.

I did not have to travel back to Dunstable in a removal van. My father considered that my arm still needed protection. So I went on the train with Mum, Dad and my new baby sister, who was six weeks old. As we were about to leave, our cat, Whiskey, scrambled up a tree and refused to come down. 'Leave it there,' said Dad, 'We've got to go now.'

Jill and I started to cry. 'But there will be no one to feed him,' said Jill.

'Someone will take him in,' said Mum, and the van trundled off. As I walked down the road between my parents, I looked back and saw a black and white face peering at us through the leaves of the tree. Abandoned.

Chapter 7: On the Move

When Aubrey and Violet discovered that the newly built Dunstable house still wasn't ready, the builder, Henry Summerfield, took care of the problem.

'You can rent Lancot House for a few weeks, Aubrey. It's round the corner from your new house and it's empty at the moment. The owners have gone abroad and are still making up their minds whether to sell it. I've been in touch with them.'

Mum was pleased. Lancot House was an imposing building. It filled me with awe as I was not used to houses which stood in their own grounds, with enough bedrooms for everyone. It stood in a grand area, so as several scruffy children tumbled from the removal van, the neighbours twitched their curtains in horror.

I gazed mystified at the row of bells in the kitchen. 'They've been disconnected, but a few years back they would flash or ring for the servants to answer,' Roy said, grinning. 'In those days it would have been nearly time for you to go into service.' I looked anxiously at him. I had read about the lives of the poor at the turn of the century and knew that seven-year-old girls could become maid servants. Dad had several dour books on social history: we all read anything that came into the house.

The back garden was thick with sycamore trees, shrubs, a large pond and hiding places. Even today I recall it as a place to dream and play.

Less than a month later, we moved down the road to our new home. I loved the airiness and the beautiful parquet wood floors. A long room ran the length of the house, and at a furniture auction my father had bought a solid oak sideboard and dining table. A cloakroom and large kitchen led off a square hall, large enough to be another room. Upstairs were four double bedrooms: Mum and Dad had the biggest, the boys shared one, Jill and I had the third, and the fourth was Shirley's. There was a cot in there too, for the baby, as Shirley looked after her if she woke in the night.

Outside, lay a field, not a garden, a bleak sight, waist high grass littered with building debris. Dad tackled it with a scythe, but it defeated his efforts. He couldn't afford to hire cutting and digging machinery.

Living on the edge of a wood, Roger, Roy, Jill and I spent as much time as possible outside, running wild and ragged, climbing trees, making dens, playing endless games of cricket in a large clearing, with a tree for stumps. We wandered for miles, coming home exhausted and hungry.

In the autumn we scrumped apples; at Christmas we went carol singing to buy Christmas presents for our parents and each other, and learned that wealthy people are not necessarily generous. So we made our way to the back streets of Dunstable, where we did better. The roads were ill-lit and had a sense of menace with shadows taking on grotesque shapes. Tony and Shirley did not come on these expeditions for they had started work: Tony in the Westminster Bank, Shirley in a newsagent's shop. We made a good team as we all had sung in school choirs and our voices blended well. The boys insisted that we sang a carol all the way through, and never knocked on doors afterwards. If no one came after a couple of minutes, we moved on to the next house. Sometimes, people came hurrying down the road after us. 'Why didn't you knock?' Occasionally we would be offered hot drinks which the boys always politely declined because that would have meant involvement and awkward questions, anathema to a Darby. I wanted to say, 'Yes please.' My fingers were frozen. I longed for a hot mug.

One bitterly cold evening Roy and I went carol singing. It wasn't long before my toes and fingers were numb, but Roy said that we must stay out longer: 'I've told Mum we'll give her what we earn tonight, so we must stay out a little longer. But I'll make you warm again, I promise.' He made me jump and swing my arms and we laughed at how stupid we must look in the middle of the street. Gradually the blood began to flow freely once more, painfully at first, then with a satisfying glow.

Warm again, we finished our singing, earning a substantial amount, and ran laughing and happy to the steamed- up windows of the fish shop. Then we smothered the treat with salt and vinegar.

'Last December, in Felpham, Mum ran out of money mid-week,' Roy said on the way home, 'Dad was in Luton, working, and then the electricity meter ran down, and it was dark and cold. Don't you remember?'

I shook my head.

'Tony and Shirley went carol singing until they had got enough for some shillings for the meter, and money for chips for tea,' Roy said. 'Eating these chips reminded me.'

We started to run through the black, icy streets, and the money in Roy's pocket clinked in time to his jogging. I laughed as I grabbed his jacket. 'You're Tony, and I'm Shirley, and we're taking money for the meter home to Mum.'

'We'll never be as good as they are, Jude, not if we live to be one hundred.'

He was right.

We could no longer afford the Lancot Avenue house which had been built to Mum and Dad's specification. It remained without gates or garden walls, the overgrown field becoming daily more dishevelled. It was a fine house, vastly superior to anything we had lived in before. Mum thought it was beautiful, especially the spacious kitchen, although she didn't like being on the edge of woods and downs, for she found them creepy. Lights blazed in our house when dusk fell to offset her fear of darkness and the unknown.

However, finance and fear had caused yet another move.

Our parents had seen less of the Summerfields in the Lancot Avenue house even though they finally had a home in which they would be proud to entertain. They could not afford to do so, nor could they afford to go out drinking. My father told people that we had to go back to the coast for his wife's health, and that we would settle permanently in Sussex. Although Mum's health was reasonable at the time, and she had recovered well from the pregnancy and birth of her eighth child, his words proved prophetic.

Less than a year after moving to Lancot Avenue we were on our way back to Sussex, this time to Bognor Regis. At the beginning of July, 1951, we children clambered back into a removal van, and off we went to Bognor. Roger returned to Chichester High School, this time accompanied by Roy. Jill and I went to a different primary school, Westloats, and Tony was called up for National Service.

Shirley began work in a fish shop, but a few weeks later she had to leave as Mum fell ill.. She was admitted to St. Richard's Hospital in Chichester, towards the end of September, with dangerously high blood pressure. Her condition was so worrying that the doctors decided to use experimental drugs on her, and confined her to bed. It was a month before the doctors reluctantly allowed her home again, with strict instructions about her medication, which she ignored.

Every Sunday evening while Mum was in hospital Shirley gave Jill and me a pencil each and piece of paper, to write to her. My letters were full of mundane facts:

Shirley has washed my jumper to make me clean for school tomorrow. The baby sleeps all night and that means Shirley does too.

Jill's approach was much more creative:
It is Sunday evening and we are sitting on the floor in front of the fire, which is crackling and spitting. Outside it is cold but we are cosy and warm.

I missed my mother, although life was calmer at home with Shirley in charge. With Tony in the army and Dad in Bedfordshire from Monday to Friday, she was looking after five children ranging in age from fourteen years to eighteen months. She was fifteen.

Each weekend Mum would send one penny bars of Cadbury's chocolate home by Dad for the children. Shirley would give them to us on Monday morning to take to school to eat at playtime. Violet was never as loving as when she was away from her children. She showed our letters to the patient in the next bed, a headmistress of a primary school, who delighted Mum with her praise of the writing.

'Only Mum would not realise that the poor woman was being polite,' said Roger.

Mum came out of hospital on 26th October, 1951, the day after the General Election which swept Atlee's Labour Party out of power and re-instated a minority Tory government under Churchill. Jill and I played in the back garden to stay out of Shirley's way while she made the house shine for Mum's homecoming. Every now and then we would run to the French windows for Roy to give us the thumbs up, for in the early stages the Labour party seemed to be winning. We didn't understand anything about politics, but Dad was a fervent Labour supporter, which meant we all were.

Mum felt well when she came home as she had been resting for four long weeks. Because she felt so strong she ignored all the doctor's warnings and was soon spending most of her evenings in Bognor, playing bingo. It became another addiction, and she spent some of the money Dad left for the mortgage payments on this new type of gambling.

Shirley began working as a telephonist, and her mother took all her money, saying she would pay for her clothes. That meant Shirley had a few shabby garments for work, and however desperately she washed and pressed them, they looked scruffy. The lack of money at home meant that Jill and I went to school in clothes that were dirty and didn't fit. But each morning before school and Shirley leaving for work, we cleaned the house until it sparkled.

I became friendly with a girl in my class called Jenny Paston, a pretty, petite, fair- haired girl. We had a friendly rivalry to come top in the frequent class tests, and as the class was sat in order of achievement, it meant our desks were next to each other, which increased our friendship.

Jenny Paston's father taught in the adjoining secondary school, and one day after lessons she took me over to the staffroom to meet him, as he had stayed behind marking. I recognised his look of disgust as he eyed me up and down, taking in my tangled hair, my boy's shorts, and my sandals with the sole coming off.

The next morning I ran up to Jenny, as she stood chatting to some other girls in the class. She held her nose and then said, 'Oh dear, here comes the dustbin. My father says I'm to stay away from you in case I catch something.'

The other girls giggled in delight. 'Dustbin, dustbin, Judy Darby is a dustbin.'

For days I endured the taunts, then asked Roy for advice. 'If you were a boy you could thump her,' he said, 'but girls don't do things like that. Just ignore it.'

Jenny Paston's campaign of playground and classroom terror continued for weeks. I stood alone, isolated and humiliated, until one day, something snapped.

It was a day when our dog, Lassie, was moulting freely. Our mother could not stand the hairs everywhere, and each morning Jill and I would get down on our hands and knees to remove the hairs from the carpet with damp cloths.

Mum called down the stairs from her bed: 'Shirley, it's 9 o'clock. Let Jill and Judy go to school now.'

We sprinted up the road, and as we ran, Jill straightened her clothes and pulled back her hair from her face, plaiting it. She then fastened the plait with an elastic band. I did not have her dexterity or an elastic band, and so my fine, untidy hair flopped over my face and shoulders. Dog hairs clung to my clothes and my knees were grimy.

I walked into the classroom where young Mr. Huntley was already calling the register. Tall, slim and energetic, he would stride past our house every morning and evening on his way to and from school. Sometimes he overtook me, without acknowledgement, as I struggled home from the shops with a heavy bag. Usually this was in the morning as our local grocery shop was always open by 7:30 a.m.

The week before he had had the class miming different situations. 'Judy, come out here and pretend to be carrying a heavy bag of potatoes.' I did so, and leaned over towards the imaginary weight.

'Oh, go and sit down,' he said. 'I'd have thought that you of all people could have got that right.'

Now he paused from calling out the names, and sighed. 'Judy, it's about time you learned to get up in the morning.' Then he gave a sardonic grin as if enjoying his joke.

I muttered an apology and slid into my seat, aware that the girls were nudging each other and whispering. I tried to push my blouse into my shorts and pick off the worst of the dog's hairs. I heard a girl sniggering behind me and Jenny Paston edged away. 'Do I have to sit next to a dustbin? It smells.'

At playtime I stood alone on the asphalt, as far away from my classmates as possible. But a group of girls, led by Jenny Paston, made their way over to me. I pressed my back against the warmth of the brick building, and watched them approach.

Jenny Paston looked sideways at her friends, and said, 'You wear boys' shorts.'

'Pam wears shorts, too,' I said.

'Yes, but hers are girls' shorts, proper shorts, not something that her brother's thrown out.'

The other girls were giggling, as she continued, 'Your shorts are dirty and torn, and covered in dog's hairs. You're an animal, a dog. Perhaps you've got fleas.'

Her friends squealed. 'Judy Darby's a dog and has got fleas.'

For one brief moment I looked at Jenny Paston. She stood there, confident, immaculately turned out in her pale blue dress, white socks and polished Clark's sandals. Her fair hair was a shining halo. She was everything I longed to be.

Something snapped. I stepped forward and slapped her round the face with tremendous force and all the passion, hurt and anger of the weeks of torment.

She gasped in amazement and pain, then holding her bruised face, began sobbing loudly, running into school in search of a teacher.

The school did not give me a formal punishment but asked me to account for what Mr. Huntley termed, 'the behaviour of a guttersnipe.' I stood in the musty, rank smelling headteacher's room, head held high to keep the tears at bay. 'It's wrong to call people names, Sir. She called me 'dustbin' and it was the only way I could stop her.'

The head pointed out that two wrongs didn't make a right, and I accepted that. He told me that Jenny Paston wouldn't call me names again, and said I could go back to lessons. I made for the door with a lighter heart, but as I turned the handle, he said coldly, 'Ask your mother to mend your shorts.'

I felt as if he had hit me.

Back in the classroom, no one taunted me again. No one spoke to me either. I was left alone with my shame, and my longing to be like the other girls with their clean, pretty dresses. I coped by working hard to make sure I beat Judy Preston in the classroom tests. She hated me for it. I didn't hate her: I wanted her to accept and like me, as she had done before her father saw me, but I knew that she never would.

Jill and I were at our grubbiest and most unkempt during our time in Bognor. When our mother was in hospital Shirley washed our clothes and kept us tidy, but once Mum took over the household again freeing Shirley for work, we wore the same scruffy clothes every day. Tony remembered us coming down the road to meet him one day, looking like ragamuffins with the soles flapping off our sandals. The toes had been cut out so we could get more wear out of them. We were cleaned up for a family photograph in the back garden at Bognor, but Jill's skirt and my dress had uneven hems.

That was the year that Tony bought his brothers and sisters toothpaste and toothbrushes for Christmas. Mum was not at all shamed, and showed no interest in these gifts. We loved the novelty, but once the toothpaste had gone, no more was bought. My mother had false teeth and soaked them each night. I know Dad had a toothbrush but I never saw him with toothpaste. Grandma had taught Shirley to use a finger and salt, so that would have been Mum's training, but she didn't see fit to pass it on to her children.

The house was still scrubbed daily.

I think Mum barely existed at that time, skating on the surface of reality. She tried to ignore the escalating debts, terrified Dad would discover how much she owed, and that even the mortgage was not being paid. He could not afford to give her much, and she had always been an appalling manager. Ill, tired and depressed, she ran away from her responsibilities and took refuge in bingo.

Out of school, life was good. We were encouraged to leave Mum in peace once the housework was done, and so we spent hours on the beach. In the summer, a man with a Punch and Judy show held weekly talent competitions. The audience clapped each act, and the volume of clapping determined first, second and third places. I always entered, reciting a poem, and usually won a shilling, probably more for my waif like appearance than any talent. Always hungry, I then ran over to the fish shop, whose rich smells made my stomach growl in anticipation. Happily I stuffed chips into my mouth.

At Christmas there were presents for everyone with plenty of food. That year in Bognor, I woke up to find a stocking full of little gifts like pencils and socks, and at the bottom of the bed there was a carrier bag containing a doll in a green and white knitted outfit, a red shoulder bag and some books. Jill had similar presents, and the day passed in a haze of joy. Dad cooked a chicken, Shirley prepared heaps of vegetables, and with the chicken Dad served the suet pudding he made every year, boiled in a cloth, and then sliced. It was difficult to move afterwards.

But on Boxing Day the rows began over money. My father was perplexed as to where it was all going. He knew Shirley was paying for her keep and Tony was sending money home from his meagre army allowance.

'You don't give me enough, I can't manage,' Mum said.

'I work my guts out from Monday to Friday in a foundry. I have no more to give you.' Dad's voice was quiet as he ran his fingers through the little bit of hair he had left. The younger children looked at each other and disappeared upstairs to play Monopoly. The voices came floating up the stairs.

'You're living it up in Dunstable and at my mother's all bloody week. You're not here to run the house and look after the kids.'

'Hardly living it up. Your mother hasn't two pence to rub together but she manages a damn sight better than you do, and the kids look like urchins. Not much looking after there.'

Upstairs the four of us exchanged glances. It was cold outside, but infinitely more peaceful. We crept downstairs towards the front door.

Upstairs the four of us exchanged glances. It was cold outside, but infinitely more peaceful. We crept downstairs towards the front door.

Bognor Regis 1951
Back row left to right: Shirley, Roger, Dad, Mum and baby Valerie, Tony.
Front row left to right: Jill, Judy, Roy, Lassie the dog

It was Mum's idea to take in paying guests to help with finances. 'People will pay good money to get a breath of sea air.'

Dad was sceptical. 'Where will we put them? We haven't got an inch to spare.'

But Mum had it all worked out. The main bedroom upstairs would be given to the guests, with the front room downstairs used to serve their breakfast and evening meal. They could also use that room as a sitting room in the evenings, and would be expected to stay out all day.

Tony was in the army, called up for National Service, so Roger and Roy could fit into the tiny third bedroom. Mum would have the second bedroom during the week, joined by Dad at weekends, and we four girls could sleep downstairs in the back room which would double up for family living in the daytime.

We only had the one bathroom but managed. The bathroom was only used for infrequent baths: all other washing, whether it was for clothes, vegetables or bodies, took place in the kitchen.

Mum didn't conduct her boarding house activities for long but while she did so the money was useful. A frequent visitor was Charlie, who lived in Luton, and had known Mum and Dad for some time. He was getting on for fifty, single and never seemed short of cash. He made me shudder to look at him for he was oily, plump and sweaty, with a flushed face and jowls.

It soon became clear that he liked Shirley, and his sunken eyes would follow her round the room. He always asked where she was when he came in from his days out in Bognor, reeking of alcohol. Shirley hated him, and even at sixteen she realised that there was something sordid about his interest.

One evening I went to bed even earlier than usual. I had been out in the sun and had a headache. The other children were out playing, and Shirley was not yet home from her shift at the telephone exchange. I lay on the big bed in the back room, drifting in and out of sleep. The evening was warm and languid, and outside, the sound of children playing and calling dimly entered my consciousness. I could hear the squawk of gulls, and imagine them circling round the sandwiches left on the beach. All was peaceful, and even my throbbing head seemed to ease.

I heard the kitchen door open, and roused myself thinking Shirley had come home. Then I heard my mother's tinkling laugh and the deeper tones of Charlie. The tap was turned on and there was the tinny splash of water into the kettle. Kitchen chairs scraped and it was clear that Mum and Charlie had settled down for a cup of tea.

'Vi, I'll gladly lend you some money. And you're insulting me by asking me to keep it secret from Dabber. As if I would say anything.'

'Charlie, you're a real friend. I don't know what I'd do without you. But I'll pay it back as soon as possible, I promise. I wish I could do something for you.'

I heard Charlie clear his throat. 'Tell you what, Vi. I'd like to take young Shirley out for the day. She's a lovely girl, like you my dear, and she's sweet and innocent.'

Mum gave her laugh. 'I like to think she takes after me. Actually, people often say we're more like sisters.'

Charlie's answer was polite. 'Oh, I can see that Vi; you don't look half your real age. But I'd like to give Shirley a treat, and that would be like treating you, wouldn't it? I know you mothers like to see your children happy.'

There was silence for a moment, and then Charlie continued smoothly,

'You're such a good friend that I'm not pressing for the money back.'

Mum's answer was drowned by the boys slamming through the back door, and I turned over, trying to get to sleep despite the noise.

I thought no more about the incident until I heard Shirley and Mum rowing.

'I don't want to go out with him. I don't want a treat. He's slimy and he gives me the creeps.'

'He's a good man, and he's trying to be kind,' Mum yelled back. 'And he's lent me money, so I'd have thought that it was the least you could do.'

'Let's ask Dad what he thinks, when he comes home at the weekend. I'm sure he won't force me to go out with that horrible old man.'

Crack. Mum's hand whipped across Shirley's face. 'You cunning little cow. Don't you dare mention this to your father, and if you tell him Charlie's lent me money I'll swing for you, I swear it.'

Three days later a white-faced Shirley and grinning Charlie left the house early, on Shirley's day off. Two hours passed and they were home again, Charlie grim-faced. Shirley rushed into the back room and slammed the door.

'What happened?' my mother asked. 'What's wrong, Charlie?'

'She kept saying she felt sick, even started retching at one stage. I had to bring her back.'

'Never mind, Charlie. Perhaps another day, soon.'

'I don't think so, Vi. Look I've decided to go home today, after all. I'll just get packed. And you won't forget to send me that money as soon as you can, will you?'

That evening Shirley lay in bed, crying. I eased myself closer. 'What's wrong, Shirley? Are you ill?'

'No. I'm all right. Jude, it was horrible. We walked along the beach and he tried to take my hand. His hand was so sweaty it was dripping. I pulled away from him, and he leaned closer, and his breath stank. I didn't have to make it up about feeling sick, I don't why I wasn't sick there and then.'

Every Sunday evening my mother and Shirley went to the railway station to see Dad off for the working week. Directly the train had been waved into the distance Mum would take Shirley to the pier to see if there was a new show, and, failing that, the bingo which Mum loved.

It had been several months since she had made any mortgage payments, and one morning a letter arrived threatening re-possession if the total arrears were not paid off.

Mum panicked. 'What are we going to do? How am I going to tell Dabber?' After two distraught days she decided to write to him in Dunstable.

He confronted her that Friday night, after he arrived home for the weekend, tired and distraught. 'What the hell are we going to do, Violet? Where will we live? I suppose we'd be eligible for a council house back in Dunstable.'

His voice tailed off. We all knew his dream of settling in Sussex. He loved the sea. The weekly treks between Bedfordshire and Sussex had taken their toll and he was looked old before his time. His experience in the terrible smog as he crossed London one Friday night to catch the train at Victoria, had left him with a hacking cough, not helped by his work in the foundry, and he regularly choked up evil coloured phlegm. He had decided when he left Lancot Avenue to look for a job in Sussex. Each weekend he scanned the local papers for a suitable job.

Now, he sat slumped in his chair, facing yet another financial crisis.

'Most nights you go out to play bingo,' he said, 'it eats up the money.'

'I do not.' Mum flared up in anger. 'What's Shirley been saying?'

Dad laughed without humour. Rolling a cigarette, he paused before he answered. 'Not Shirley: misplaced loyalty there. She won't say a thing. No, I asked Jill and Judy. They're too young for deception. You haven't managed to train them yet.'

Jill and I tried to make ourselves invisible as our mother shot a vicious glance in our direction. Then she swung round on Dad, fists clenched by her sides as if resisting the urge to punch him. 'What else is there to do in this god-forsaken hole? And I need to do something to help me forget that you made me get rid of my baby.'

Her voice rose, ugly and penetrating. He turned from his contemplation of the fire, looking shocked. 'You've got a baby,' he said, 'you love her.'

A deep silence settled over the room as we all held our breath. It was broken by a harsh cackle from Mum. 'You stupid man, you bloody stupid man.'

The next morning our father looked old and grey faced, as he stood in front of the fire he had just lit.

'Violet, what do you think of my council house idea, in Dunstable? I'm sure we'd be eligible after all our years living there. It would be a decent size.' He gave a reluctant chuckle. 'One advantage of having ninety-seven children.'

'A council house? You've got to be joking. I would never live in a council house.'

'No, you'd rather live on the streets, and that's what is likely to happen.' My father coughed and directed a stream of phlegm towards the back of the fire. Then he sat down and put his head in his hands. 'Somehow I've got to get us out of this hideous, bloody mess. But Violet, you've got to learn to budget, and not spend money we haven't got.'

Tony was home on leave and he and Shirley exchanged glances.

Later that day my father raised the council house idea once more, and received a stream of abuse in return. We younger children tried to make ourselves scarce, and on Sunday morning he took Tony and Shirley for a long walk along the beach. Their mother had confided in her eldest children for years, treating them as adults long before they had any maturity, but this was new for him. He discussed the options but it was soon obvious what he intended doing, and it severely hurt his pride and self esteem.

'There's no real choice,' he said, 'I'll have to go to Gerry, cap in hand.'

Gerry Bagshawe owned the foundry where Dad was foreman. He had always been a hands-on employer, who had worked alongside Dad in the foundry in the war when there was pressure to make caterpillar tracks for Bren gun carriers and conveyor belts for Royal Ordnance factories. There was mutual respect between the two men, particularly as Mr. Bagshawe had been grateful to my father when he had used his considerable influence to break a strike. Dad had told the men that Bagshawe was a good, fair employer, and that to bring the foundry to its knees was counter-productive.

On another occasion the two men had been trying to mend a furnace when Dad changed hands to get at an awkward screw. Gerry Bagshawe nicknamed him 'Two-hand Dabber', because of his dexterity.

My father went back to Bedfordshire earlier than usual that Sunday evening. He said he wanted to be on his own to think. The next weekend we learned that he had phoned

Gerry Bagshawe when he arrived at Luton Station, to arrange a meeting for early Monday morning at work. We never heard the full details of the conversation between the two men, but we knew that Bagshawe would pay off the building society and sell my father one of the houses owned by Bagshawe Conveyors. He would also lend the deposit for the house. The loan would be interest free, taken in instalments weekly from Dad's wages. One proviso was that Mr. Bagshawe would personally be responsible for making sure the mortgage was paid to the building society, for two years, so that Mum and Dad became used to the pattern of payments. The house would be reasonably close to the foundry, so that Dad could finally settle down without the weekly travelling between Sussex and Bedfordshire.

'You've been a bloody fool, Dabber,' was Gerry Bagshawe's final comment. 'Keep your eye on the family finances, and don't leave it to your wife.'

My father came away feeling deeply shamed. He respected his employer, and up until then that had been mutual. Now he was told that he couldn't be trusted financially.

Ironically, when he told Violet the news the next weekend she was thrilled. 'If Gerry Bagshawe is supplying the house, I expect it will be grand.'

'Don't be so bloody stupid; will you never learn?' Dad spoke harshly. 'He knows exactly what I earn and what I can afford.' Kicking a stray log to the back of the fire with more force than necessary, he added, 'And I expect he'll factor your spending prowess into the equation as well.'

My mother wasn't listening. Her disappointment when she first saw the house in Shakespeare Road was like a child's. She came back home to Bognor in tears. 'It's horrible,' she said.

'It's not horrible at all,' said my father. 'It's a perfectly decent three bedroom semi, with a good size garden and a garage. Violet, I keep telling you, there won't only be a mortgage to pay; there will also be the debt owing on this house.'

'The road's not made up,' said Mum. It's a mass of stones, and there's a field opposite the houses.'

'The road is navigable, and will be done in due course,' said Dad. 'What's more, the field opposite is a bonus. It means we don't look out on other houses.'

I listened to all the exchanges between my parents. Nothing was ever kept secret. But all I understood was that we had to move again, back to Bedfordshire. I felt glad that the tension had gone out of the air and that I could leave the hated Westloats School and go back once more to the school I loved, Evelyn Road.

I marvel now at my father's extraordinary patience. Bagshawe Conveyors was a place where men admired him, including his employer. Now his sordid family finances had been revealed and he felt bitterly ashamed. Yet we never heard him reproach our mother again for the mess. Perhaps he agreed with Gerry Bagshawe that he had been a fool to leave the paying of debts to her, and must take some responsibility.

Once more we started packing.

Chapter 8: Musical Festivals

In 1951, the year we lived in Lancot Avenue, Dunstable Town celebrated the Festival of Britain with a musical festival. It consisted of various classes, playing musical instruments, singing, and elocution. Elocution was a vague term which covered poetry recitation, and for younger children, reading a previously unseen page from a famous piece of literature.

Mum thought this was wonderful. She decided to coach Jill and me for the poetry competition for our age group and entered us for the sight reading too. 'You've always got your heads in books. Now you can show that it's been useful.'

So she paid the entrance fee of two-and-sixpence, and we began the laborious practice. Every evening we had to stand in the corner of the room – 'Stand straight, head up, don't slouch,' – and recite *Mary* by Walter de la Mare. The poem gave me no joy, and what was worse, I didn't understand it. I vaguely knew it was about being hungry. 'You don't need to understand it,' said Mum. 'Just put expression into the way you recite it.' Then she would demonstrate and I would mimic, and another dreary half hour would pass.

Dad was asked to listen and criticise. 'Dabber, I think they are beginning to recite it quite well. What do you think?'

From behind his paper Dad muttered, 'Yes, very nice. Now go and recite it in the garden. That will keep any intruders out.'

A few weeks before the competition a letter arrived, saying that Jill was just a few days too old for our class as she had recently celebrated her ninth birthday. It was too late for her to be entered for a higher one, and so she was reprieved. Mum re-doubled her efforts with me, panicking that she might be teaching me in the wrong way. She sent me off to school on the appointed day, clearly worried, and said she would telephone Miss Greenwood to see if I could leave school early. That way we would be sure of getting to the Town Hall in time for the elocution competitions at 5 pm.

In the afternoon I received a summons to Miss Greenwood's room. 'Have you done something wrong?' whispered the girl next to me, eyes large, as I left the class.

Miss Greenwood sat at her desk on the far side of her room, a tall, slim woman in her early fifties. Her hair, with its ordered permed curls was a silver grey, and she wore the slightest touch of powder and lipstick. She always wore a smart tweed costume, under which was a twinset and pearls. Her shoes were elegant, highly polished heeled lace-ups, with stockings of sheer silk.

'Come in, Judy.' She was smiling and my spirits rose. 'Your mother is worried about the competition tonight. She has asked me to listen to you. Now, head up, stand straight, clear diction.' It could have been my mother talking. Then she took me round all the classrooms and I had to recite *Mary* in each one of them, children gawping and nudging each other. No seven-year-old was ever better prepared but how I hated it. When I reached their classrooms I could see that Roy and Jill were equally embarrassed.

Miss Greenwood let me go home early, and as I hurried down the road from the bus stop I could see Mum looking out for me. She had been shopping and bought me a new red check school dress, red sandals and white socks. There were red ribbons for my plaits. I was thrilled. 'Oh, Mum, I know I'll do well in these clothes.'

'Well, make sure you do.'

The Town Hall was full of excited, anxious competitors and their families. I looked at the stage. It looked huge and magnificent with its draped, dusty curtains either side. I didn't feel nervous.. Despite all the preparation I still wasn't quite sure what was happening. Soon my name was called with a list of others, and I had to leave Mum and go behind the stage to the large ante- room. There I waited with the other competitors. Some struck up conversations but I sat there going over and over the poem in my head, feeling comfortable in my vivid, scarlet clothes.

'Judith Darby, you're next.' I scrambled to my feet and followed a harassed-looking woman with a list. We climbed the steps which led to the back of the stage and I could hear a faint murmur of voices. 'On you go,' hissed the woman, and I walked out on to the stage and faced a packed audience. I could see Mum's worried face halfway down the hall. At a desk in the middle of a cleared space, sat a woman, who smiled a plastic smile.

'When you are ready, my dear,' she said, and picked up her pen.

The actual recitation was an anti climax and the unseen reading was a familiar passage from *Alice in Wonderland*, so not unseen by me. I won both classes and the adjudicator wrote on my poem appraisal form, 'You really made me *feel* hungry.' Mum was overjoyed. 'I knew I had got it right. I should have gone on the stage.' I had never seen her so happy and sparkling. This mood lasted until after the prize winners' concert the following Saturday. Miss Greenwood was in the audience and as the audience trailed out at the end of the evening Mum sent me to show the headmistress the plaque and certificates I had been awarded. Miss Greenwood was effusive in her praise, and beckoned Mum over. 'This is wonderful. Judy is a good advertisement for the way Evelyn Road School teaches its pupils to have excellent diction at all times.' Mum beamed, and all the way home she laughed and sang as if she were under the influence of some strange narcotic.

But it wasn't to last. The next day her mood came crashing down. Ecstasy for Mum meant an inevitable descent into depression. This time she did not seem to be able to lift herself. Was she reflecting on the lost dreams she once had to go on the stage? Was the imminent move to Bognor, and the weekly separations from Dad, gnawing at her? Was she mourning the loss of the dream house which she had helped plan? Perhaps the decline in health which hit her so sharply two months later was already making itself felt. Whatever its cause, the depression manifested itself in a withdrawal from her children's needs and welfare.

A month later we moved to Bognor Regis and eighteen months passed before we saw Bedfordshire again. We returned to the area to Shakespeare Road, Luton, and this was to be the last home where we all lived together as a family. We had moved four times in less than four years, yo-yo-ing between Bedfordshire and Sussex.

I missed the sea, but was delighted to be back at Evelyn Road School. The downs, Leagrave Marshes and the surrounding countryside were compensation for the loss of the beach, and we were free to roam to the marshes to collect fat, black comma tadpoles, and wander over to Bluebell Woods, bringing back the musky blooms. 'Don't plant any bluebells in the garden,' warned Dad, 'Otherwise they'll take over.' I liked that idea but would not have dared disobey. And although the first sight of the silent, blue carpet of the woods always filled me with a joy that caught in my throat and teased my eyes, away from there the flowers lost their lustre and magic, as if pining for their natural home.

That Easter, coronation plans and excitement swept through Britain. Along with streets all over the country, Shakespeare Road planned its party. It would be on the field opposite the gently curving line of houses, which had a view uninterrupted by the bungalows which were built a few years later. Every week, one of the coronation committee would knock at the door, collecting money, and Dad always gave, although he had to have a token grumble first about Royalist nonsense. Some of the men cordoned off part of the field, and at regular intervals mowed it ready for the children's races. My father was bemused by this. 'Why don't they leave it until nearer the time, rather than do the same job over and over again?' The answer was an enthusiasm, which he lacked, for all things royal, and also to be seen to be playing one's part, something else he declined to do.

In Luton Road, our old neighbour, kind Mrs. Coombes, paid towards *her* street celebration. She put in extra each week so that Jill and I would be able to go to that party too. Her reasoning was that the Darbys had lived in Luton Road for twelve years and were entitled to join in the fun. When Dad heard this he raised his eyebrows and said, 'Depends how you define fun. But if Mabel wants to waste her money on Jill and Judy, it's up to her. She can afford it.' We were thrilled. From the Shakespeare Road party we received a coronation mug, and a spoon from the Luton Road one. It didn't take many weeks before our precious mugs were broken by careless family use, and the spoons disappeared into the sparse cutlery drawer.

The carefully tended grass opposite the Shakespeare Road houses was left forlorn, as it poured with rain on the day of the party, which had to be held in the hall of the local secondary modern school. In the days that followed the party my father appeared to grow anxious about the patch, shorn and lonely in the middle of the wild, knee high grass, buttercups and dog daisies. 'Get out there and play cricket. Don't waste all their efforts.'

At Evelyn Road Miss Greenwood produced a special Empire Day service and I read the speech given by Elizabeth on her twenty first birthday:

I declare before you all, that my whole life, whether it be long or short, shall be devoted to your service...

By this time I was getting used to reading incomprehensible prose, and had learned that if I adopted a solemn expression and read loudly and clearly, strictly honouring the punctuation, adults would say, 'She's very young but reads with such understanding and expression.'

Mum had gained a fresh vitality since returning to Bedfordshire, and although Jill and I rarely had new clothes, we never looked like the urchins we were in Bognor. As I would be centre stage in the Empire Day celebrations, Mum bought me a second hand white dress which Shirley washed and starched.

Afterwards, all the children who had taken part were introduced to the Mayor. He looked at me with a wry expression on his face. 'I remember your brother Roger in the school victory parade after the war.'

Everyone remembered. Each child held up a Union Jack as they marched round the playground to the sound of 'Land of Hope and Glory'. But Roger held up a huge, blood-red flag with a swastika on it. Our family couldn't afford a flag, so Roger had borrowed one.

The Musical Festival in Dunstable had become an annual event. Mum was anxious that Jill and I should both take part in 1953. This time she ensured that Jill was entered for the correct age group and rehearsed both of us again. The set poem for my age group was *A ship sails up to Bideford* by Asquith. Dad read the poem and commented on exploitation by 'the Empire on which the sun never sets.'

Mum no longer asked for Miss Greenwood's advice; previous success had given her a confidence which was justified when both Jill and I won.

But Mum's triumph was pyrrhic. She had now seen the child she swore she could not bear to see, a baby of whose gender she had been ignorant. My father and the doctor had merely told her that the child was well. Mum was forced to confront the decision she had made seven years previously; within hours she descended into an abyss from which she never escaped. In later years, my father often said, 'In the depth of winter the sun still shines above.' My mother was the contradiction of that philosophy.

By the time Shirley and I reached home that evening, my father had already made a decision. Silence on the subject. He believed that Jill and I did not understand the significance of what we had seen. Jill was certainly confused and ignorant of the truth. I said nothing: I had promised Shirley, but I could not get the strange girl's face out of my mind. Her happy smile invaded my dreams and I knew that I would never forget her.

Mum was ill for a fortnight, her headache so intense that she couldn't raise her head from the pillow without vomiting. Dr Aston called in daily, and after one of his visits, I heard Mum say to Shirley, 'He says that my illness was inevitable, that I can't take the shock.' She began to cry. 'I read those papers when I came home. She is mine. I can't bear it.' And the vomiting began again. Shirley held Mum's head until the retching stopped, bathing her face afterwards with a warm flannel.

I said nothing at all, to anyone, not even Shirley, but the next year Jill and I were entered once more for the Musical Festival. Stricken as she was, Mum wanted to see her daughter again, forced herself to go through the inevitable pain and sickness which followed each time.

For the next two or three years, until the annual Musical Festival was held no more, Jill and Judy Darby, and Judy Woods, dominated their classes. In one sight reading competition we three sisters found ourselves in the same class, as that year the age group for each class was extended. We took first, second and third places. It meant that Judy Woods did exceptionally well, as the age range was five years and she was the youngest.

Mum was not the only person affected by these events. Judy Woods' adoptive parents kept the programmes from these festivals and ringed the names of Judy and her two sisters, sisters of whom Judy herself was unaware.

There was also the year when Judy and I were in different poetry classes and both winners. At the prize winners' concert the compere took our hands and led us on to the stage. We sat on chairs on opposite sides, and took turns in reciting our poems to a warm, generous audience.

I kept my distance as we waited to perform through that long evening. I was too frightened to talk to this little girl, and could not get my head round the fact that she was my sister. I tried not to look at her as we sat behind the scenes.

Mum never asked if I had spoken to Judy Woods. When each Festival was over she would be ill, and look pale and withdrawn for weeks. Nothing seemed to register with her, but she would make cryptic comments directed at no one: '*All* my children have done well in the poetry competition.'

I began to dread the Musical Festivals. Mum would rehearse us with frenzy and became ever more critical of our efforts. She had made her decision to see her daughter each year whatever the emotional cost, and I can only imagine her renewed sense of loss when the festivals finished.

Chapter 9: Misrule

As Tony and Shirley grew to adulthood imperceptibly the dynamics shifted in the Darby household. It would be some while before Mum realised this, and on the surface life was settled. Once the Dunstable Musical Festivals, or eisteddfods, came to an end, Mum no longer had to endure her self-imposed annual torture.

The Festival experience which had awoken the trauma she had suffered when she had given up her child, was now given an extra, ironic twist. Mum had suddenly seen her daughter. Never again could she take comfort in ignorance, for now there was an appealing, animated face to torment her.

As Tony, Shirley and Roger were all now working, finances became easier. Mum, unable to bear her own company in the daytime, went back to work after a six-year break. She took a job at a petrol filling station, and seemed to enjoy it, becoming friends with the woman who worked the alternate shift: 'Sandy is cheerful and fun. She makes me laugh when I can manage to understand her Scottish accent.'

Mum was physically stronger than she had been for a long while, and Dad also seemed more at ease, coming to terms with his shame over Gerry Bagshawe and the loan. They began to go out with Sandy and her husband, Bob, on Saturday nights and Dad was delighted to find that Bob shared his political views.

For two years we had holidays in Kent, near Dungeness, and although there were bad moments when Mum and Dad rowed, as a family we played cricket on the beach, swam in the cold English Channel and climbed Dungeness lighthouse. The landscape was bleak and unwelcoming but that meant it attracted few visitors, which suited our insular family. In the evenings we played

Monopoly before Mum and Dad went out for a drink to the pleasant little pub two hundred yards away. No longer was Dad the inevitable winner at Monopoly as his eldest children had developed skills that matched his. In the pub Mum chatted away to strangers who responded to her magnetism, while Dad was content to put in the occasional word until alcohol made him verbose. Both came back to our rented bungalow in good moods.

'Dabber, that tall chap with the glasses couldn't believe that I was forty-three.'

'Couldn't he? His friend was an intelligent bloke; he agreed with me that co-ownership is the only sensible way forward.'

The first child to break away from the bundle of sticks and assert his independence was Tony. His disagreements with Dad over politics caused tension in a household where Dad's pronouncements were law. Mum worshipped Tony, and for the most part he was careful not to upset her. But he rarely gave Dad the same respect.

He remembered an incident which shamed him. One day he had walked in on a row between Dad and Mum. She sat sobbing at the kitchen table, head in hands, and her wretchedness moved Tony to anger. Opening the back door, he grabbed Dad and threw him outside. 'Don't you ever dare bully my mother again.' Years later he said, 'Because I was several inches taller than Dad, and twenty-years-old, I thought I was invincible. But the old man was tremendously strong. He could have knocked me into next week. He didn't. He did and said nothing. I knew how Mum would make it look as if she was a victim when she had instigated a row so I should have known better.'

Interesting points arise from this story. Firstly, the strong hold and influence Mum had over her children, even when we had often witnessed her antics and had been at the receiving end of her deviousness and irrationality. No one had seen more of this than Tony, yet he reacted strongly to her apparent distress without stopping to find out what had led up to it. Secondly, for Dad it was a replay of the scene when he had thrown *his* father out the door for his treatment of *his* mother. The irony would not have been lost on him.

Dad was proud of his eldest son and on Tony's twentieth birthday put the following letter in his card:

Dear Anthony

Congratulations on this, your 20th birthday, and may you prosper and grow in stature as the years unfold. May you never lose faith in yourself, but always believe that for you, success is your just due.

Look upon life as a game to be played to a finish, play well, play fair, and enjoy it.

Pity others, but never yourself, be temperate in all things, and remember, that in the depth of winter, the sun still shines above.

Good luck, Good health, God bless, From –
Mum, Dad, Shirley, Roger, Roy, Jill, Judy, Valerie
x x x x x x x x

Sometimes Tony asserted himself by acting in a way which invited criticism. He left his job at the bank, defying Dad's fury, and was out of work for several weeks. He said that he had done as his parents had wished all his life, had handed over most of the money he had earned, and he would now make his own decisions. This was delivered in a quiet, reasonable tone, and his parents did not know how to reply. Had Tony shouted and sworn they would have felt on safe, familiar ground, but Tony had learned how *not* to conduct an argument, and never to put himself into a situation over which he had no control.

At times this was amusing, though often only in retrospect. One of those was the ceremonial cleaning of a neighbour's doorstep.

Mrs. Wilkinson frightened me, even though by the age of ten I was familiar with the bizarre. Her eyes were hard and unblinking, x-raying the object of her gaze. She stood squarely, with her laced up shoes sitting meekly on the end of her cruelly veined, sturdy legs. Her ample form bulged with the hand-knits which were wrapped round her. A flowered overall was tied fiercely round the ensemble. Even the headscarf which topped it all was fastened under her chin with a hard, uncompromising knot.

Mrs. Wilkinson had four children, and each afternoon, hot or cold, they would group with their mother, by the front garden gate, in an unnerving stillness, looking up the road, waiting for their father to turn the corner. Each of her children wore a knitted balaclava, whatever the weather. I never knew how long the hair of each child was, for all I could see was a knitted helmet. The helmets came in rainbow colours for their mother knitted constantly as she stood at the gate each evening, waiting for her husband to come home from work. She never looked down at her racing fingers; her eyes always fixed on the horizon.

When my father first saw her, he muttered, 'My God, Madame Defarge.'

One Sunday morning our dog got out and defecated right in the centre of the Wilkinson's doorstep. Mrs. Wilkinson didn't bring her knitting with her as she charged up the road. The entire Wilkinson family advanced, although Mr. Wilkinson looked reluctant as he trailed some yards behind. My mother opened the door in response to the violent banging.

'Your fucking filthy mongrel has shat all over our doorstep, and if I had my way I'd rub your bloody nose in it!'

She got no further because my father interrupted in a deceptively quiet tone which caused his children, waiting and listening at a safe distance, to shiver. That tone was a prelude to his hooded eyes sparking and flashing, his tongue protruding from between his teeth, his massively strong hand being raised in retribution. But all he said was, 'Mr Wilkinson, I will not discuss this matter until you send your wife home.'

'Home!' shrieked Mrs. Wilkinson, 'I'm not going home until I've had my bloody say.'

My father ignored her and turned again to her husband standing miserably hunched in the background. 'Send the virago home,' he said, 'and then I'll talk to you.'

'Go home, dear,' pleaded Mr. Wilkinson. 'I promise I'll sort this out.'

His wife gave him a look of contempt and started to scoff, 'You...' Then she caught sight of my father's face and something in his expression stopped her. She gathered up her children, and backed towards the gate.

Safely there she blustered, 'Everyone knows what you sodding Darbys are like; you're the talk of the neighbourhood.' Nearing her own gate she remembered the dog's misdeeds, and her final outraged shaft echoed up the road, 'And it did it on a Sunday.'

Once Mrs. Wilkinson was gone, my father and Mr. Wilkinson quietly came to an agreement. The step would be cleaned. Much relieved, Mr. Wilkinson scuttled off. My visibly shaken mother asked Tony to clean the doorstep. He considered for a moment, and then said, 'Right, of course I will, but I'm not going to let that harridan leer or gloat from behind her filthy nets. So I do it my way.' Then he sent Jill and me running round the house gathering up any receptacle that might hold water. This collection was then filled with warm, soapy water, laced with the San Izal disinfectant beloved of my mother.

Outside it had begun to rain, a grey, seeping, drenching winter rain. Tony lined his brothers and sisters in order of age outside the front gate and briskly allocated the assorted buckets, bowls and jugs. A military walk down the road to the Wilkinson's house followed, with Tony at the head clutching *The Observer* and a yard broom. With a flourish and as much gravitas as could be summoned when clearing up dog muck, Tony wrapped the newspaper round the offending pile, removed it from the step, then ordered, 'Shirley...Roger...Roy...Jill...Judy...'and each stepped forward with water and swilled the doorstep. Tony swept the water away, and a doorstep, which had never had such thorough ministration before, gleamed and smelt fresh and wholesome.

From behind the nets Mrs. Wilkinson gaped, and Tony gave her a polite bow before marching us back the way we had come. My father was furious about *The Observer,* for he hadn't read it yet. Tony said, ' *The News of the World* would not have sufficed, Father; I needed something sober and respectable for such an important task. '

Shirley found it much harder than Tony to break away from Mum's control. But finally they both escaped through marriage. We younger children watched the battle between Mum and her eldest children's new influences from the sidelines, dreading the day that we would lose the protection offered by our sibling-surrogate -parents.

Tony met his girlfriend Anne Mills when he was head choir boy at the Priory Church Dunstable. 'I was in the Guides,' Anne said, 'and when we went to services, I would sit in the front pew and gaze at him.' She was a slight, fair-haired, blue-eyed girl, gentle and calm, nine months younger than Tony. When we moved to Felpham Mum advised Tony to break off the relationship. 'It's not fair to her,' she said, 'you can't leave the poor girl waiting in Dunstable.'

Three years later Anne and Tony bumped into each other again in Dunstable.

Shirley met Bill one Saturday evening. She had been with Mum and Dad when they had driven out to a country pub. A group of American servicemen were there, and a handsome young man detached himself from the group and came over to talk to Shirley. The attraction was mutual and immediate.

Mum wasn't keen on either Tony or Shirley becoming serious with anyone, but there was little she could do about her eldest son. He came home only to sleep, and often stayed at Anne's house. The Mills' household was ordered and serene, competently managed by Mrs. Mills, a kind lady who treated Tony with the same care as her own children. Even his washing was done at the Mills' house, so he was always turned out immaculately.

Tony always said that it was Anne's sweetness, fastidiousness and peaceful nature which had attracted him. She never raised her voice, was non-judgemental, and although Mum frequently threw nasty comments at her, Anne did not react.

Tony still gave Mum generous board money, even though it cost her nothing to keep him. After leaving the job at the bank he went to work for a leading estate agent. He proved to be a brilliant salesman, and as he coupled this with an ethical approach to selling houses, was extremely successful. Potential clients asked if he could handle their purchase: 'My friend told me that Mr. Darby pointed out what was wrong with a house they wanted to buy. I want someone honest like him.'

In the evenings Tony began studying for his chartered surveyor and auctioneer examinations, shut away in a peaceful room in the Mills' house.

Every now and then Mum's fury would erupt over Anne's influence over Tony, and she would swear and shout at both of them. 'You think you're bloody clever, keeping my son away from me,' she shouted at Anne. 'He's *my* son, and don't you forget it.'

Dad would remonstrate, 'Leave it, Violet,' but she could not control herself or be controlled when she was angry or upset.

Anne never retaliated, but occasionally Tony would turn on Mum. 'If you can't keep a civil tongue in your head and treat Anne with courtesy, then I'll move out altogether.'

Mum realised he meant it, and for a time peace would settle. But Dad was often mischievous when Tony wasn't there. 'She's brazen,' he told Mum, 'she'll do anything to lure Tony away from us.'

Roy glanced at me and held up the dictionary. In an undertone he said, 'It means made of brass.' We looked at each other bemused.

I felt confused. Anne was always kind to me, and I thought that if Tony liked her she must be nice. But, at eleven, I was still too young to separate myself from parental views.

Shirley's Bill also suffered. Mum had far more power where Shirley was concerned, and exercised it. At first she tolerated the friendship, but became concerned as it deepened into something stronger. Shirley was only allowed out with Bill on Mum's say-so, even though she was eighteen.

Dad made it clear that he disliked all things American: 'Bloody Americans are arrogant fools.' When Mum was in a bad mood she would shout at Shirley in front of Bill, 'Don't think you're going out until that ironing is done. There are more important things than gallivanting with a fancy man, my girl, and don't you forget it.' Bill stood there uncomfortable and embarrassed.

When demobilization loomed for Bill, he wanted to take Shirley back to America. But Dad would not hear of it, and Mum had hysterics. Dad said, 'Don't worry, Violet. I'm going to tell the lad that if he really cares for Shirley, he'll go back to Missouri for his demob. Then he can get a job, save up and come back to England for her.' He smiled. 'He won't be back, Violet, you can depend on it.' As Shirley needed parental consent to get married, she and Bill were forced to agree. They never considered going to court to get permission.

For a while Mum seemed to be reassured, but when Roger received his call-up papers for national service, her uncertainties and fragility reasserted themselves. One night, when Shirley was out with Bill, and Tony was at the Mills' house, she took her fears out on Dad. 'I won't lose Tony and Shirley, no one is going to take them away from me.'

Dad sighed and got out his Golden Virginia. As he rolled a cigarette he looked thoughtful. 'With any luck Tony will come to his senses, and you've got no worries about Shirley once Bill has gone back to America.'

'That girl will take Tony away. Just like you took my baby away from me.'

Dad looked startled. 'What the hell are you on about?'

'You know what I'm on about. I've had seven, eight children for you, and you made me give away my baby.'

Dad got up, strode to the door, and kicked it open. We heard the front door slam, and an uneasy silence fell over the room. I eyed the door, wondering if I could escape. But it was too late. Mum turned on me. 'Don't just sit there, you little cow. Get that kitchen cleared up, and do it properly. I'll inspect it when you've finished.'

Bill went back to America where he was demobilised from the US Airforce. He wrote to Shirley every day, telling her he was saving hard to return to England to marry her. Mum urged Shirley to have a good time and forget him. 'After all, you don't honestly think that he's sitting at home, moping for you? No, he'll be out with all the girls, a good looking chap like that.'

Shirley didn't listen.

Chapter 10: Mourning and Marriage

1956 was a year of loss. At Easter, Grandma West died. Mum couldn't face the funeral so Dad represented her. Outwardly the sadness didn't seem to affect Mum. She comforted herself with the fact that she paid the coalman the small amount that Grandma owed. 'My mother would have been grateful for me paying off her debts; she didn't like debt.' The irony was lost on her.

I missed the gentle, old lady. Despite living in poverty she had always been kind and generous to the Darby children. When Shirley and Bill had visited her every week in the back street council house with its small living room and scullery, they always took her a fish and chip supper. Shirley noticed how Grandma carefully divided her portion into two so that she would have a meal for the next day.

In the school summer holiday Mum was at work, so when the housework was done Jill and I were free to go out with friends. Mostly, Roy and I played cricket, or Monopoly, when it rained. He said I could be Freddie Truman because I bowled fast, and tactfully overlooked the fact that I could only bowl underarm. He said he was Lindsay Hassett, the Australian captain. We talked about living together when we were older, and I would keep house for us and cook egg sandwiches for breakfast every day. I had a preference for bacon, but Roy was vegetarian, so that would be out.

I think of that school summer holiday of 1956 as the last golden time of my childhood. Paradoxically, the weather was cool and thundery. But I was content, something more to be desired than happiness, free from anxiety and tension. Free from the dread of having to stumble out excuses for not having dinner money *again*, not having the correct equipment , not having to explain why homework wasn't done without giving away that housework was the reason; free from being regarded as an idle, thoughtless pupil. In a class of girls wearing crisp, white blouses, wielding Scheaffer or Parker pens, I felt scruffy and inadequate. With the absence of school, for a few, brief weeks life was good.

However, there were times when Roy and I loathed each other and fought like maniacs; I would end up bruised and battered. It seemed quite normal behaviour to us. I hid my bruises from Mum, but as she would have taken Roy's side I needn't have bothered.

That summer Roy introduced me to stories that I thought of as being for boys, but he laughed at me. So I waded through Scott, Stevenson, Verne and Huxley, and enjoyed them. I was confused by Dr Jekyll's dual personality and asked Roy to explain evil to me. Despite his sixteen-year-old certainty about the consequences of evil I was still bewildered. 'Have I got an evil side then? If it grows stronger will I die?'

Roy grinned. 'You're so evil that you'll die tomorrow.' I felt stricken but he laughed. 'For goodness sake, Jude, remember what Dad says when Mum is worried about death: "Only the good die young, you'll live to be one-hundred-and-fifty."'

Two months later I remembered his words.

We had gone back to school in September, when Tony said, 'Anne and I are getting married in February.' Dad muttered about a 'bundle of sticks,' but he did go to see Mr. Mills and offer to help pay for the wedding. He was relieved when his offer was refused, but annoyed by the manner of the refusal, a terse, 'I don't need any help in paying for my daughter's wedding.'

Mum looked depressed, and her mood became even more unpredictable.

Then Bill wrote to Shirley to tell her that he had saved enough money to return to England to marry her. When Mum had recovered from the shock she said that they must begin married life living with us; they could have the back room made into a bedsitter. Tony privately told Shirley, 'You'll be raving mad if you agree to such a thing.' But she found it difficult to tell Mum, especially as Mum considered that Shirley would be delighted with such an arrangement.

In early October Bill came back to England, and the day was one of pure Darby farce. Mum and Dad were always late for everything, and although Shirley had been up before dawn to clean the house to Mum's exacting standard, she had to wait hours for them to get ready. Mum insisted that she and Dad should go too. 'You can't go to that dangerous place on your own. You don't know what type of person you'll run into: foreigners doubtless.'

Shirley grew increasingly anxious. 'We're going to be late. It will take nearly two hours to drive there, and his plane is due to land in an hour.'

'Then he'll just have to wait, won't he? With any luck he'll turn round and go back again.' Mum said tartly, and Shirley was afraid that if she answered, Mum would deliberately slow down.

By the time they finally left the house Shirley was in tears.

Dad was a poor navigator; they got lost and there was no Bill waiting at Heathrow. He had waited over an hour, then decided that they weren't coming, so he travelled to Luton by train, and caught a bus to Shakespeare Road.

Dad's car drew up outside Shakespeare Road three hours after Bill had knocked on the door. In the meantime Jill and I had made him tea, and engaged him in polite conversation, although at first I found his accent difficult to understand.

'I wrote to Shirley with the exact time of the flight's arrival,' Bill said.

I laughed. 'If she could, Shirley would have gone very early this morning and waited patiently. You've got a lot to learn about this household, Bill.'

Bill looked thoughtful. 'I sure have, Judy.'

The wedding was booked as soon as Bill arrived in England. Although he had saved hard, he would need a job before long, but by law in 1956 he would be unable to seek work until he was married.

Money was scarce and so a white wedding was out of the question. Caxton Hall was mooted, and other socially popular venues, but it all came to nothing. Shirley would marry in Luton Register Office, like her parents before her. The date was set for the first Saturday in November.

One Thursday evening at the end of October, I came home from school, washed up the lunch dishes left by Mum and Dad, and prepared to leave the house to go up to the Mills' for a bridesmaid's dress fitting. Anne and Tony's wedding had been fixed for the following February and Anne and her mother were making Anne's dress and those for seven bridesmaids. Roy hadn't arrived home and I assumed that he had stayed behind at Dunstable Grammar School for a game.

After the dress fitting I played with Susan, Anne's youngest sister, and waited for Tony to give me a lift. When he finally came, he had Val, my six-year-old sister with him. He was not his usual chatty self. Seeing my enquiring look, he turned away, but his hunched shoulders and grey face worried me.

Tony didn't speak, but Anne said brightly, 'Roy has had a slight accident; he's in hospital. Judy, you and Val are going to stay here tonight.'

I wanted to ask, 'What happened? Is he in pain? When is he coming home?' but no words came. I looked from one to the other, desperately trying to read the signs. Suddenly the warm, friendly house had lost its appeal. I wanted to go home. I needed to be there when Roy arrived, to welcome him and check for myself that he was all right.

Then Tony spoke, his voice harsh, 'Come on Anne, we'd better get back,' and they disappeared, leaving me bereft. Mrs. Mills said, 'Goodness, look at the time. I think bath and bed are in order. And I'll make a nice cup of cocoa.' Her cheerfulness sounded false, and it also discouraged questions. Soon I lay in the dark, tormented by visions of Roy lying still and white in a hospital bed.

Roy   August, 1956 aged 16

On the school bus the next morning I sat on my own by the window, gazing unseeingly at the familiar shops and houses. The road snaked away down the hill towards the hospital which held Roy captive. As the bus rumbled by I turned my head away.

I sat mute, stiff, upright and miserable. The other girls' laughter and conversation washed over me, easing in and out of my consciousness.

Then the words 'accident', 'grammar school boy', and 'bike' roused me from my self-absorption. 'It was horrible,' the girl said, shuddering, 'blood everywhere.'

'How much blood? Was he dead?'

'Don't know. The police wouldn't let us get close enough to see. But a man said the poor lad didn't stand a chance being mown down by a lorry that size. Another man said that it was the boy's fault as he was overtaking on the nearside.'

I wanted to shout at them, to tell them to shut up, to hit their silly, ignorant faces. Instead I dug my nails into my palms and stayed silent, and felt as if I was betraying Roy.

The school day passed in its usual frenetic whirl of thirty five minute lessons punctuated by the strident bell. In the lunch hour I took myself to the far corner of the grounds and sat in the late October sunshine, hidden from view in a damp, mossy dell. I could clearly see the veins in the dying leaves, the whorls on the brittle bark of the trees, could hear the scuffle of small creatures in the dank, rotting undergrowth and the sigh of the dying breeze.

Reluctantly, I obeyed the bell's summons to afternoon lessons. I did not want to leave my sanctuary. But I struggled to my feet, touched an oak tree to wish Roy luck, and ran back across the grass with twigs and leaves clinging to my school tunic.

During last lesson a school secretary opened the door. 'A message for Judith Darby: she's not to go home tonight, but back to the Mills' house.' With a nod to my teacher, she closed the door, her high heels clicking away down the corridor.

Everyone turned to look at me. I avoided the inquisitive glances.

Miss Dorling, tall and pencil slim, clapped her hands. 'Since when has Judith become an object of curiosity? Let's get back to work.'

In the Mills' home that evening I faced silence about Roy, but everyone was kind. I listened to conversations from the next room or in the hallway, but any allusions to Roy were far too cryptic for me to work out. I was used to the overt playing out of emotion and anger, and did not understand subtleties.

I played with Susan that evening, and at times almost forgot my anxiety. But once in bed visions of a maimed Roy danced before my eyes. When I could stand it no longer I crept from the bed and switched on the light. I had to read; books were what I had always used to banish disturbing thoughts.

In the adjoining bed Susan didn't stir. In her protected happy world there was little to disturb. I helped myself to the first book to hand and noticed it was by Enid Blyton. I could hear Roy's scorn: 'She writes rubbish, choose something better,' but crawled back into bed, where I read until the words blurred and my eyes grew heavy. Finally I slept.

The next morning at breakfast, Mrs. Mills said, 'Judy's father is coming to collect her and Valerie soon.'

'Oh,' said Susan, 'I'd hoped we could go to Saturday morning pictures.'

'Another day,' said her mother brightly, and I sat there, breakfast untouched, looking round for clues on people's faces.

Dad and Tony arrived together, both looking older, grey and grim. I got my things together and then scrambled into the back of Dad's Austin A40, next to Val. Tony sat in the front with Dad, and the five minute journey home was passed in total silence. We turned into Shakespeare Road, three hundred yards from home, and Dad drew the car to a halt. Outside the sun struggled to make an appearance. Inside we sat united in an unspoken hell.

Dad turned in his seat and looked at Val. Tony looked straight ahead. I felt invisible, not part of the tableau before me.

'Valerie,' said Dad, his voice almost inaudible, 'Do you know where heaven is?'

She nodded, six years old and uncomprehending.

'Roy has gone to heaven,' said Dad.

He turned back to the wheel without a glance in my direction, saying, 'Keep your spirits up, Judy,' then drove to the house.

I found out the details much later. When Roy was rushed to hospital, they operated to remove his spleen. The next day he recovered consciousness and spoke to Mum.

'Mum, am I dying?'

She took his hand. 'No, of course not. Why do you think that?'

'I heard the nurse say so.'

Mum tried not to cry. 'You're not going to die.'

Roy smiled. 'Will you tell Dad it wasn't my fault? It wasn't.'

Later that evening they took him to the operating theatre again, to attempt to fix his arm which was fractured in several places. The hospital didn't know he was asthmatic, and his heart couldn't take the strain of another operation so soon. He died late that Friday evening.

I have clear memories of the funeral, cameo performances played out by the characters. Dad, Tony, Roger, and my Welsh cousin Norman carried the coffin high on their shoulders. Their suits and highly polished shoes were impeccable, their shirts crisp and white, with the black ties stark against the brilliance. I tried not to think of Roy lying white and still inside the coffin, nailed down against his will. We sang *He Who Would Valiant Be*, the Evelyn Road School hymn. Miss Greenwood attended the funeral, and came back to the house afterwards and sat upright on a hard chair in the corner of the room, clutching a bone china cup and saucer borrowed from next door. Mum told Jill and I to go over and shake hands with her. Although I had left her school over a year previously, I felt the familiar fear in her presence.

There were many people to shake hands with that day, and I longed for them all to go home so I could take the false, aching smile from my face. I could tell that Dad felt the same way, but Mum derived a strange comfort from being surrounded by so much sympathy and attention.

The day after the funeral Mum said, 'Of course, Bill must go back to America. He can come back next year, or sometime later.' She waved her hand vaguely.

Shirley's head jerked up in amazement. 'Mum, he's staying, and what's more I'm still going ahead with the wedding. It will be quiet, without a party. God knows, none of us feel like celebrating, but we need to get married before Bill can get a job.'

Mum screamed. Dad came rushing in to see what was wrong. 'Violet, are you all right?'

'All right, of course I'm not bloody all right.' Mum clutched her chest, gasping for breath. 'Dabber, tell her Dabber.'

'Tell her what?' Mystified, Dad looked from Mum to Shirley.

'She thinks she's still going to get married. Tell her she's not.' Mum clutched at Dad's arm. 'She's a wicked, evil cow to think of getting married at this terrible time. Send that Bill back to America, Dabber, back where he came from.'

Dad looked nonplussed, and Shirley stood there helpless under the attack. Bill moved over to her and put his arm round her shoulders. 'Postponing the wedding won't bring Roy back,' he said. 'If it would we'd willingly change our plans. But there's no point. After all, there'll be no reception or party.'

Mum looked at him with venom, and then took refuge in tears, rocking backwards and forwards in her chair, head in hands.

'Violet, I know this is hard for you,' said Dad, 'but there's no logic in postponing the marriage. The man needs to get a job.' He put his hand on her bowed head, and she jerked upright.

'Don't you think I'm being punished enough? Roy has been taken from me because you made me give up my baby.'

'Here we bloody go again.' Dad's voice was no more than a mutter, but we all heard it except Mum, who cried out in pain, 'I've lost my son and I don't intend to lose my daughter. Dabber, please send him back to America.'

When Tony came home, Mum appealed to him, but he saw no point in delaying the wedding either. 'Look, Mum, it's not as if they're going to have a wonderful start to married life, poor sods. It will be a basic ceremony in a cheerless register office. The least you can do is give your blessing and wish them well.'

But Mum had power and intended using it. In 1956, consent of both parents was required for a child under the age of twenty-one. Shirley would not reach that age for another two months. When the papers were produced for Mum to sign, she refused.

'I want him to go back to America,' was her constant refrain. Tony pointed out that air fares were far from cheap, and that it had been impressive the way Bill had worked to save so much so soon. 'Mum, do you know anyone who has the money to fly to Scotland, let alone across the Atlantic?'

Mum screamed at Tony in response but he was undeterred. 'Neither of them would have chosen to be married at such a time, but there's no point in cancelling it now.'

At the last minute Dad slammed the consent form down in front of Mum. 'Sign the bloody thing, now.' Shocked, she obeyed, and then Dad grabbed it back before she could tear up the form.

Dad handed the form to Shirley, and said grimly, 'Well, you've got your way; I hope it makes you happy. You've certainly broken this bundle of sticks.'

Shirley, white with shock, looked as if he had hit her.

Then the question of where Shirley and Bill should live could not be avoided any longer. Tony tried to talk them out of living at Shakespeare Road, and offered to find them a flat to rent while they saved up for a property of their own. This seemed like a dream to Shirley, but Mum would not hear of it, and Shirley felt too exhausted to fight further.

The back room downstairs would be given over to the newly weds as a bed sitter. Mum and Dad and five children would sleep upstairs. When you overcrowd animals, trouble starts…

There was nothing wonderful about the drear November day when Shirley married. Mum insisted that Shirley should do housework up until an hour before the ceremony. Shirley rushed round, and put on the dress Mum had ordered she should wear. Mum took her time getting ready, and it was soon obvious that they would be late.

'Please, Mum, please hurry up.'

'I'll take my time. If we're late, we're late. It would be a good thing if they tell us we'll have to come back another day.'

Dad turned round from the kitchen sink, his face covered in lather, razor in hand. 'You don't mean that, Violet, you know you don't.'

By the time they reached the register office, their turn had gone, and the registrar had ushered the next couple in. Shirley and Bill were fitted in at the end of the day's proceedings. The only people present were Mum, Dad, Tony and Anne. Then the newly married couple left for a brief honeymoon near Dungeness, a forsaken spot next to the desolate lighthouse.

At the time I only knew Keats through poems like *Meg Merrilees* and *Ode to Autumn,* but a few years later I studied his poetry as part of an A Level course. A shock of recognition flooded through me as I read:

> *As with us mortal men, the laden heart*
> *Is persecuted more, and fever'd more,*
> *When it is nighing to the mournful house*
> *Where other hearts are sick of the same bruise.*

The Monday morning after the wedding, I stood at the bus stop by the Luton and Dunstable Hospital. The morning was bleak and raw. Several other people were waiting for the bus, including some local girls, on their way to work, aged about eighteen. They were whispering together, obviously about me, first furtively, then more boldly. I felt uncomfortable under their scrutiny, and started to edge away, clutching my satchel close to me. Suddenly, one of the girls spoke to me loudly, making sure everyone waiting for the bus could hear.

'Your sister got married on Saturday, didn't she?'

I remained dumb.

'Well she did, didn't she?' the girl persisted.

The whole queue was listening, and I felt trapped, as if I had been caught in some murky misdeed. Panic made me voluble. 'She had to get married.'

I paused, as even in my innocence, I knew what that comment meant colloquially in our neighbourhood. So I stumbled on, 'Bill needed a job, he needed work, she had to get married.'

It was no use. Miserably I turned away, and pretended not to care as they began to discuss in tones I was intended to hear, how the boy wasn't cold in his grave. They couldn't have known about Hamlet, otherwise doubtless the queue would have been entertained by the funeral food gracing the wedding table.

My cheeks burnt until they stung as distress washed over me. It wasn't my shame alone that gnawed at me; it was the terrible ignorance shown about a family brought low by grief, and the cruel infliction of hurt.

I didn't take the experience home: I knew better than that.

Tony married Anne the following February, three months later. If any of the neighbours considered this was too soon, gratefully I didn't hear of it. It was a totally different affair. I was one of seven bridesmaids; there was a packed church and lavish reception. This was Mr. Mills' eldest daughter's day: the child he adored was to marry in style. And the Rector of the Priory Church came out of retirement to marry the young man who had been his head choir boy.

I think my parents enjoyed the day. In the evening, after bride and groom had been cheered on their way, there was a party at our house for my parents' friends. Shirley cleaned the house beforehand and prepared the food; Jill and I helped.

At the wedding reception Bill bought me a fizzy drink, and talked to me kindly as if I mattered. I loved him for it.

I knew that Shirley and Bill living at Shakespeare Road wouldn't work. Mum treated Shirley as if she was unmarried and at her beck and call. Shirley recalled:

My mother still expected me to run the house as I had done for most of my life. On one occasion she would not allow me to go out with Bill and his friend as the ironing had not been completed. Another time I arrived home from work and took off my dress to change. There was a small window between our room and the kitchen, and my mother frequently peered through it. Seeing me standing there in my petticoat, she shrieked to my father, 'She's stripping in front of him, the brazen hussy.' This always amused Bill, and in later years he would often refer to me as his brazen hussy.

The tension was not good for their marriage, and as the year turned to Spring, Shirley finally snapped. She was washing a white jumper at the kitchen sink one evening when Mum marched into the room clutching navy school knickers. 'Val needs these for school tomorrow,' she said, and shoved them deep into the bowl so the water turned navy and the colour crept into the white wool strands.

Though later Shirley saw this as such a small matter, at the time she could take no more. Crying and shaking she ran into her room and packed her suitcase with her few clothes. Then she ran out of the front door and made her way to Tony and Anne's spacious bungalow, situated at the foot of Dunstable downs.

Tony phoned Bill who was working on nights at Vauxhall Motors, and told him to come to their home the next morning.

And there, despite Mum's tears and protestations, Shirley and Bill remained, until they had saved enough to put a deposit on a new maisonette. Shirley made her peace with Mum and she and Bill spent two happy years in England before deciding to move to Missouri, where Bill had lived until joining the U.S. army.

Chapter 11: Dark Days

When Shirley and Bill decided to make their home in Missouri he went on ahead to find a home for them. That meant Shirley reluctantly moved back to Shakespeare Road for a few weeks. Tony and Anne would have made her very welcome in their home but we all knew that Mum would raise hell if she thought she was being snubbed. Shirley said, 'It wasn't worth the fight.'

Jill and I quickly became used to having Shirley around again, acting as a buffer between us and Mum. With her usual quiet efficiency Shirley slipped seamlessly into the role of doing most of the housework, and it was a time of deceptive peace.

I was not prepared for the terrible wrench when she finally left. Tony took her to the airport and I watched the car disappearing up the road, yard by yard, getting smaller and smaller, and felt that something warm and safe was going out of my life for ever.

Mum emphatically refused to allow Shirley to have some friends round for her farewell evening. Shirley had tiptoed around Mum. 'Mum, do you think I could ask Margaret Tully and a couple of the other girls round for a couple of hours, next week, when I leave work?'

Mum frowned. 'It would only be for coffee and some snacks. Obviously, I'd supply the coffee and snacks, Mum.' Shirley added quickly, 'And I'll get it ready, and clear up afterwards.'

'No, I don't want you to have your friends here.'

'Remind Mum of all that you do for her, tell her that it would be nice to be on the receiving end for a change, ' I whispered to Shirley. She could have gone out for a meal with her friends, but Shirley was again paying Mum board as well as buying a plane ticket. In 1958, eating out in Luton was rare and expensive.

Mum's unhappiness at her departure meant she became increasingly critical of Jill and of me. Her demands grew daily. Each morning, her insistent call came at six am. Propped up on her pillows, after a restless night, Mum would be eager to hear noise and bustle about the house. So Jill and I struggled down the stairs to begin our chores. It wasn't so bad in summer, but in winter it was still dark and our toes turned to ice on the cold lino of our bedroom floor.

I would turn the wireless on to the Home Service, so loudly that the adjoining neighbours must have been able to hear. But it was important that Dad could hear it too, with its frequent time checks, so he could judge his leap from bed to get to Bagshawe's before the hooter went. I knew more about current affairs than anyone else of my age group at school, because I listened to the BBC to relieve the monotony of the housework.

Still in our nightclothes we began work. Jill would make a start on the living room, raking up the ashes from the night before, often burning herself on coals that still glowed.

It wasn't easy to clean that room as you had to edge round the furniture which was too large and cumbersome. The oak sideboard and table had been bought for the bigger room at Lancot Avenue and were crammed in together with a brown leather three-seater and two armchairs.

Over the sideboard hung a hunting scene. This was strange, as Dad was opposed to fox hunting, and was fond of quoting Oscar Wilde: 'the unspeakable in full pursuit of the uneatable.'

In the kitchen I would fill the kettle and light the bloody- minded gas ring which stood on a tin tray, which in turn was perched perilously on a stool beside the sink. I would stick a piece of torn newspaper through the hole in the gas geyser to get a light from the pilot. As the newspaper flared up, I would hold it to the gas ring, already belching out gas from where I had turned it on. On bad days I managed to burn myself, or worse, the gas refused to light. Mum would shout down the stairs for her tea, fighting to be heard over Jack de Manio's not-so dulcet tones on the wireless.

When you turned on the geyser which supplied our hot water, flames would shoot out of the top, hitting the ceiling, a soot stained testimony. How there was never a terrible accident is beyond comprehension.

After I had made the tea, I took two cups up the stairs, tongue between my teeth as I concentrated on the task. Dad would never drink his as he preferred to sleep until the last possible moment, but the tea still had to be set carefully by his side of the bed. When I questioned the purpose, Mum said, 'I've had enough of your bloody cheek,' so I continued to take two cups up to their bedroom.

On Mum's side of the bed there was a small table crammed with the necessities to get her through the night: a lamp, a couple of Netta Muskett romances, a glass of water, a box of Newberry Fruits and a large biscuit tin crammed full of tablets, including lethal barbiturates such as phenobarbitone. They had been prescribed at times by Dr. Ashton, but she was vague and inconsistent about how and when she took them.

At 7:20 Dad would come running down the stairs, cursing as he came. He would take a swig from another cup of tea I had strategically placed on the edge of the table.

'Piss,' he pronounced the tea, and went out the door.

By this time Jill had almost cleaned the living room, and I would be washing the kitchen floor, on hands and knees, with San Izal and bleach, an evil mixture. San Izal was a coal tar disinfectant, sold for cleaning outside drains and out buildings.

Everywhere sparkled. One typical morning we checked each other's rooms to make sure that no speck of dust remained.

Jill nervously called up the stairs, 'Mum, we've done the work. Can we get ready now?'

This daily same question was followed by the same answer. 'I'll be down in a few minutes to make sure that it's been properly done,' and we watched the clock anxiously while we waited.

From upstairs came the creak of Mum easing herself from her bed, and her ponderous tread across the landing and down the stairs. What kind of mood was she in? We held our breath.

I retreated to the kitchen, listening hard, as Mum went into the living room followed by Jill who was trembling, partly from cold and partly from fear.

'There's still marks of ash in the fireplace. You haven't washed it properly.' How had we missed that when we had checked?

'This sideboard hasn't had polish on it, don't you give me that. You can get out the Mansion and do it again, using a bit of elbow grease.'

Jill started to protest, and I heard a slap. 'That's for your bloody cheek.'

There was a creaking sound as the settee was pulled away from its place. 'I knew it, you haven't hoovered here.' Mum was triumphant. 'So, if you want to get to work in time, you'd better get cracking.'

By now Jill was crying. 'Mum, please let me get ready; I can't be late again.'

'Then you should have done it properly in the first place.'

I stood in the kitchen, chewing the sleeve of my nightdress, eyes swivelling round the room, looking for possible faults with the cleaning. Mum appeared in the doorway. 'What's that stain on the table? A cup has been there and you haven't cleaned it. Does that mean you haven't scrubbed the table this morning?'

'No Mum, sorry Mum, that's from Dad's cup. I'd done the table before he came down.'

'I wonder.' She looked suspicious, and began to run her finger along the light switch. 'This hasn't been cleaned. Get it done, and you can scrub that table again. I don't believe your lies.'

'I spent ages scrubbing the table. Feel it and you'll find it's still damp. Anyway, Tony calls it the bleach board and says it's not good to eat off something that's practically held together with corrosive.'

I had gone too far, as always. Mum advanced across the kitchen, arm raised. I dodged, but she still managed to catch my hair and pull it as I cringed back against the sink. Clutching a handful, she lashed out with her other hand across my face.

'You cruel, horrible woman,' I shouted. I never learned that insulting Mum was the worst possible thing I could do. I was obsessed by the idea of fairness, and the cruelty of the situation burned me up inside. If my own children criticise me I always think about it and usually come to the rueful conclusion that they are right, but Mum had no insight, no self knowledge and in her eyes was never wrong. She often accused me of being as cunning as a wagon-load of monkeys, but I wasn't; I was naive and lacked guile. Immature for my years in every way, I saw the world in black and white.

After re-doing the tasks to Mum's satisfaction, we were allowed to have a cursory wash at the kitchen sink before racing upstairs to put on our clothes.

As we ran up the road together, I said, 'I'm starving. I haven't got any dinner money either.'

There was no one waiting at the bus stop, for the rush to school and work was over. We stood there, out of breath and dishevelled, and looked at each other. 'Never mind,' I said, 'It starts all over again tonight.'

I was due to sit my 'O' levels in the summer. Finding time to do my homework was difficult. But Religious Studies, or Scripture as the school called it, was easy as we were tested on a chapter of *St. Luke* or the *Acts of the Apostles* each week. I propped the Bible behind the taps and learned it parrot fashion while washing up. In the lesson we answered a simple essay question on it, and the actual exam was no harder.

I loved History, and so did Dad, and we frequently argued about what I was learning. One evening I told him we were reading about engineers and road builders, and that I thought Thomas Telford was the greatest engineer of his generation, and he was also a road building pioneer.

'Macadam was superior to him,' my father said. I disagreed as I was thinking of the total achievements of the two men, and finally had to dodge his hand, as the warning sign of his eyes blazing and his tongue appearing between his teeth, made me realise the danger. Dad didn't understand measured discussion.

Then our young English teacher commented about ideals becoming obsessive. 'It's like the Russians with their five- year plans; they've become slaves to their own ideals.' I made the mistake of telling Dad. With a furious rustling of the paper, he sat bolt upright. 'The ignorant woman; everyone is a slave to their own ideals. For example, if a woman cleans a room she's a slave to her own ideals. Get back there tomorrow and tell that teacher so, and tomorrow evening you can tell me she's taken back what she said.'

On the way to school I pondered my problem. I didn't want to confront the teacher, and I didn't want to face Dad's anger if I didn't. I finally decided that I was more afraid of Dad. In the English lesson I put up my arm. 'Excuse me, Miss Macdonald, but my father says you're wrong…' I struggled to the end of what Dad had said, and watched uncomfortably as this young, petite woman's face turned red, and she fiddled with the chalk. But she made no answer and got on with the lesson.

That evening Dad pounced. 'What did she say?' I was ready with my lie. 'Oh, she said thank you very much, you're absolutely right, Dad.'

It was not the end of the matter. I had previously had a good relationship with Miss Macdonald. She liked my enthusiasm for English, especially poetry. I was one of the few who enjoyed the set anthology, *Rhyme and Reason*, and she often read my essays to the class. But now she seemed to avoid me, and when a political point arose in *Ozymandias* she prefaced her comments with, 'I don't want to tread on anyone's toes...' Then, one morning as I walked down the corridor, the head of physics, a tall, thin woman called Miss Peacock, stopped me and asked my name. When I gave it, wondering what trouble I was in, she said, 'So you're the little communist.' Her face was cold and disapproving.

I walked on in shame as I realised the matter must have been discussed in the staffroom.

When the time came for me to sit my 'O' levels, I would study late into the night, desperate to make up the time used for housework. The school despatched us on study leave, but there still weren't enough hours in the day. Mum liked me being at home, and instead of cleaning the kitchen at 6 am, she postponed my efforts until later so she could be up and oversee the tasks before she went to do her afternoon shift at the petrol station.

I became over tired, and one morning as Mum filled the sink with boiling water laced with San Izal and bleach, nausea flooded over me.

'Mum, I can't face it. I'll be sick.'

She made no reply but wrung out a cloth in the water and flung it at me. 'Start at that end of the kitchen, and do it properly.'

I knelt down and started washing the floor, then suddenly vomited. Mum was disgusted. 'You dirty little cow. Clear it up and get the floor washed.' She stalked towards the living room, hand holding her nose. 'Open the back door to let the smell out.'

That afternoon, after Mum had gone to work, I left the lunch dishes and curled up on the settee. I meant to stay there for just a little while, but the next thing I knew it was nearly six o' clock and Dad was coming through the door.

'Look at the state of the kitchen. Nothing washed up, and no kettle on for a cup of tea. What the hell have you been doing all afternoon?'

I had jumped to my feet when I had heard him come in, and now stood facing him. 'Nothing, I've done nothing, and nor would you have done if you felt like I do.'

No one cheeked Dad and got away with it. I hadn't got the energy to dodge the expected blow, and closed my eyes in resignation.

The blow didn't come. I opened my eyes to see him moving over to his chair, clutching his newspaper. 'I'd like a nice cup of tea when you're ready, and none of your piss.'

The summer holidays came and with them the relief from studying. I awaited the results of my 'O' levels without much interest. I knew my strengths and weaknesses very well and could forecast the outcome. In September I was due to go into the sixth form and I looked forward to that as I would only be taking subjects I liked.

Mum seemed to be quite well, but after a routine visit to Dr Ashton, he sent her to the Luton and Dunstable Hospital to see a kidney specialist. She already went there regularly to have her blood pressure monitored. But she rarely took the tablets with any consistency and refused to inject herself with an experimental drug to bring down the blood pressure. When the injections were first prescribed Dad used to do it for her, but she swore he hurt her and so stopped.

From my bedroom window I could see the hospital, a tall, wide building blocking the landscape. Shirley had worked there for a while on reception, and some High School girls worked there once they had turned sixteen, cleaning wards in the holidays. The pay was good, but when I suggested I should get a job there, thinking I could buy some clothes and a decent fountain pen - biros at school were strictly forbidden - Mum said that I was more use at home.

Mum came home from her appointment with the kidney specialist with some disturbing news. Tests had shown that one of her kidneys needed to be removed. On the positive side he thought that this might well bring down her blood pressure.

Dad was sceptical as he thought it had been raised too long, and all the experimental drugs had not worked. But he agreed that if the specialist thought it was a good idea, then perhaps it should be accepted.

Mum was due to go into hospital in late September, and as the time grew near she became tearful and wanted Shirley to come home. By now Shirley was settled in Missouri and had a baby son, but Dad wrote to ask if she would come home as Mum wanted it so much. By the time Mum packed a bag to take to hospital with her, and had been driven the short journey round the corner in Dad's car, we had received no answer.

That day Jill and I tidied and cleaned, and cooked Dad's evening meal, telling him to assure Mum that we had worked hard on the house as it would mean so much to her. He came back from visiting, and told us that her operation was the next day, and that she was upset at not hearing from Shirley.

We were upset for Mum. It is hard to explain our ambivalence towards her. There were times when I hated her, but one kind word, a radiant smile or unexpected gift of a pair of socks or a bag of sweets, and I would feel that there was nothing that I wouldn't do for her. Then there were the thoughtful gestures. In my first year at the High School Mum brought three books home from shopping, for me to give to my friends for Christmas presents. I proudly wrapped them and took them to school, thrilled when the books were received and read with pleasure.

But since Roy's death these kind acts had grown fewer, and Mum's unpredictability grew. When she was in a good mood, no one could be more understanding, and we would tell her confidences which would later be thrown back in our faces, usually in front of the whole family. Yet we never learned, and continued to long for her approval and love. We all felt the same and always clung to the hope that this time things would be different and Mum would stay in a good mood. I realise now, that without that hope, we couldn't have stayed sane, although a psychiatrist told me that it was inevitable we must have all turned out to be disturbed. And so it has proved: but all of us are affected in very different ways.

The morning of the operation an airmail letter was lying on the mat. 'Dad,' I shouted up the stairs, 'there's a letter from Shirley.'

Dad came bounding down the stairs, two at a time. He ripped the letter open and scanned the lines, the frown on his face showing his anxiety. 'She's coming home,' he said, the relief in his tone evident. 'She'll be here tomorrow.' He started making plans. 'Judy, don't go to school today. Run round to the hospital and tell them your mother must see this letter before she goes down for her operation. Then you take the bus up to Tony's and tell him he needs to go to Heathrow tomorrow to meet Shirley. She's bringing the baby with her.'

'Where will the baby sleep?' Jill asked.

'God knows.' Dad looked vague. 'Judy, when you go to Tony's, ask Anne about borrowing a cot or something. That's more her department.' His face cleared. 'Yes, she'll know what to do.' Then he noticed the time. 'Get some bloody clothes on and get round to the hospital with that letter. She's having her operation first thing.'

As I ran round the corner to the hospital I suddenly realised the full impact of what he had said. Shirley was coming home. I knew it could only be a temporary stay but my heart sang at the thought of the kind, familiar figure walking in through the back door.

At the reception desk sat a girl who had been a colleague of Shirley's. She greeted me cheerfully, but said that as it wasn't visiting time I couldn't go up to the ward.

'Please let me,' I begged. 'This letter says Shirley is coming home, and Dad wants Mum to know before she has her operation.'

The girl looked uncertain, then said, 'I suppose if I turn the other way, I won't see you sneaking past.'

Smiling my thanks I shot up the stairs to the women's surgical ward, breathing in the disinfectant smell and atmosphere. Unnoticed, I slipped into the side ward where Mum lay. She was asleep, and clearly had been pre-medicated for she didn't stir when I whispered her name. I looked at her, shocked by her pallor and the lines deeply ingrained in her face. She looked frail and gaunt. Someone had tidied her bed that morning, for the sheets were crisp and taut. I looked at their smoothness and thought that Mum would have approved.

A nurse appeared in the doorway, looking surprised and disapproving. 'What are you doing here?'

I explained, and finished, 'So you see, it might make a tremendous difference if Mum knows Shirley is coming home.'

The nurse looked bemused. But she was kind and said, 'Give me the letter. I'll make sure that if she wakes before we take her down to the theatre, that she's told.'

I held on tight to the crumpled envelope. 'But I won't know, will I? And Dad will ask me.'

The nurse sighed, and pushed a stray wisp of dark hair back under her hat. She looked tired and I felt guilty about my persistence. Then she leaned over Mum and said in a clear, strong voice, 'Mrs. Darby, we have some news for you.'

Mum's eye lids flickered and then opened. The nurse turned to me. 'Tell her.'

'Mum, it's me, Judy. Shirley is coming home.' I was shouting in my eagerness, and Mum half turned her head towards me and smiled for a brief moment.

'That's very good news.' Her voice sounded faint and hoarse as if her mouth and throat were dry. Then she closed her eyes and drifted back to sleep again.

'Thank you,' I said to the nurse. 'Thank you so very much.'

Then I ran off to carry out the rest of my instructions, thankful for being busy. I did not want time to think about Mum's operation and the fact that it might go wrong.

The day Mum came home from hospital Shirley cleaned the house from top to bottom. Jill and I helped. The time flew by, and the chores seemed almost easy as we badgered Shirley about her life in Missouri and the strange habits of Americans. She was washing the kitchen floor, and at one point straightened up and laughed. 'Judy, the way you talk you'd think Americans were an alien species.'

'Dad seems to think so.' I giggled. 'He doesn't approve of America or any of its policies. The only way we can make up for the fact that you married an American is for Jill or me to marry a Russian.'

Shirley wrung her cloth out in the hot, San Izal water, looking thoughtful. 'Then God help you. By the way, has anyone told Mum that San Izal puts a grey layer on the floor and makes it look dirty when it isn't?'

'We tell her all the time,' said Jill, 'and get in trouble for it.'

'Trouble? Why should you get in trouble for that?' Shirley looked puzzled, and I was seized by a fear that she had forgotten Mum's volatile temper, and might even believe her stories about Jill and me.

I tried to appear offhand while watching Shirley closely. 'Hit,' I said, 'with the broom or poker, or whatever is handy. I'll start on the bedrooms,' and I walked off up the hall.

Shirley came running up the stairs, drying her hands as she came. 'Jude, don't run away. I'm home now. It's going to be all right. '

'And how long are you going to stay?' By now the tears were streaming down my face. 'It will be fine while you're here. Then you'll go off again. You don't know what it's like. Why should you care?'

As I looked at Shirley's concerned face I knew I was acting like a spoilt brat. I knew she had scraped up money she hadn't got, to come to England as soon as my father had asked, bringing her baby too. How could I make her feel guilty about us? Mum and Dad had already done that about her emigrating with Bill. The old refrain had been trotted out: 'a family is like a bundle of sticks...'

'Jude, I have to go back to Missouri again. My home is with Bill now and little Billy.' She hesitated and then said, 'I don't know whether I should tell you this, because Mum and Dad would never allow it, but Bill wants me to take you and Jill home to live with us.' She ran her fingers through her hair, looking tired. 'That's how much I care.'

At 4 o'clock Dad brought Mum home from hospital. She struggled through the door and slumped on the chair at the foot of the stairs to recover her breath. 'The place looks lovely, Shirley,' she said, with tears in her eyes.

Then Dad helped her up the stairs to her bed, and she looked round with approval. Her eyes lighted on the flowers on the dressing table. 'My favourite freesias. You are a good girl, Shirley.'

The following Saturday Jill was going away overnight with the Luton Girls' Choir which was giving a concert in Hampshire that evening.

Mum sat up in bed after she had eaten her breakfast, supported by four squashy pillows, and wrote out a shopping list. 'Jill, I want you to go in to Luton for these things. I want best butter and cheese from Sainsbury, crusty bread from Bloomfields, and some yellow fish from MacFisheries.'

As Mum sat pondering over the rest of the list, fiddling with her pen, Shirley said, 'But Jill has to be on a bus to meet up with the choir by 1 o'clock. She's going to cut it very fine. It's gone ten already, and she has to get ready.'

'She should have thought of that,' said Mum, leaning back on the pillows. 'She should have got ready earlier this morning.'

'But she's been on the go since she got up,' said Shirley. She could have added that Jill and I had been running up and down stairs, carrying out Mum's instructions, since 6 am.

'Why don't I go to Luton?' I asked. 'It makes more sense. At the moment I'm just looking after Billy while Shirley is busy. Jill could do that.'

Mum hauled herself up in her bed, gasping for breath. 'See?' she said to Shirley, pointing a triumphant finger in my direction. 'See? I told you how bloody cheeky they are. I'll give you "makes more sense". Wait till Dabber comes home, he'll sort you out,' she finished with some satisfaction.

Shirley helped her lie down again.' You're a good girl Shirley. I don't know what I'd do without you. You don't know what I put up with from these two. Nothing but answering back, especially Miss Judith, the evil little cow. Dabber says she's spirited; I call it insolence. Thinks she's so high and mighty now she's doing A levels.' I walked out of the room, fighting back the inclination to shout, 'The chance to feel high and mighty would be quite something. I don't even have the time to do my homework.'

Jill left the house, running up the road, desperate to finish the shopping in time. The buses in to Luton could be unreliable and every minute counted.

I went back to playing with Shirley's baby and tried to make myself inconspicuous.

Just after 12 o'clock I heard Jill's footsteps hurrying down the side passage. She came through the kitchen door, flushed and anxious, and eased the string handles of the carrier bags from her fingers, where they had cut into the flesh. Shirley took the shopping from her and started to put it away.

'No,' said Jill, 'don't do that. Mum will want to check it first and count the change.'

The shopping was duly carted upstairs and set out on Mum's bed. Mum looked it over, muttering that the fish pieces looked a bit small, but otherwise unable to find fault. Then she held out her hand for the list and the change, and began to calculate aloud.

I was gathering up the shopping from the bed, and Jill was giving surreptitious glances at the bedside clock, when Mum said, 'There's sixpence short.'

'There can't be,' Jill said. 'I was really careful to check the change in each shop.'

'Don't 'can't be' me. I'm telling you this change is wrong.'

'Mum, Jill has to get ready as she'll miss the coach in Luton. She can't miss this concert, and it's too late for them to replace her. Remember she's doing the announcing this weekend.' Shirley's tone was calm, but her face was worried as she looked at Jill wringing her hands beside the bed.

This plea to Mum's pride in her children's achievements fell on stony soil. I realised in surprise that Mum no longer cared about that, and hadn't for some time. While I was mulling this over and wondering when the change had come, Mum's anger was growing. With her usual uncanny perception it was clear she was realising that the three daughters in front of her were on the same side, that her divide and rule policy was in tatters.

She grabbed the clock and flung it at Jill. It hit her on the forehead, and blood began to flow freely. A stunned Jill didn't even seem to be aware of the blood dripping down her cheek and into her mouth, but cowered back against the wardrobe.

Shirley was shocked. 'Mum, what are you doing? Even if the money is wrong, it will be a mistake. God knows, we all make mistakes. It's easy not to check the change properly when you're in the hustle of a queue.'

Mum's face contorted. By now she was raised up on her pillows practically out of the bed. 'You don't know her,' she screamed. 'You went away, you left me, you don't know her. She's thieved that sixpence from me. They're both as cunning as a wagon- load of monkeys.'

'Of course she hasn't stolen your money. I'll give you the wretched sixpence.' She left the room and came back with her purse. In the meantime, clutching the bag of shopping, I crept from the room, and Jill followed, holding her head.

'If you can get that bleeding stopped, just grab your things and go,' I whispered. 'Shirley packed a bag for you while you were out.'

'Take her back to bloody America with you, if you care about her that much.' As Mum's loud, angry sobs drifted down the stairs Jill and I managed to find a plaster to patch the wound. Then Jill left the house, pale and shaking. I watched her from the window as she ran up the road and felt the ice in the pit of my stomach.

Dad came home soon afterwards, and for a long while was closeted with Mum in the bedroom. When he came downstairs I stayed out of the way, but could hear his conversation with Shirley.

'Your mother is very upset. It's important that she's kept happy and calm.'

'I understand that Dad, but Jill had done nothing wrong. The poor girl was already late, and now she's had to go off with a gashed forehead and no lunch inside her. It's not right.'

'What gashed head? Whatever happened, I expect it was an accident. You don't know those girls. They're cheeky and sullen, and your mother thinks they are stealing from her.' His voice rose and I knew he would be leaning forward in his chair, jabbing a finger at Shirley. 'You should never have taken their side against her. It's all very well you waltzing in for a few weeks from America after breaking her heart by leaving home in the first place. She's terrified you'll go back to Missouri again and leave her. I can't tell her that I think you *will* go. Then to top it all you listen to the lies those girls tell you. My priority is to get your mother fit and strong again, and nothing,' - I heard him thump the side of his chair, and could picture his darting blue eyes - 'I repeat nothing, will get in the way of that.'

In the next room my head spun. A conversation was taking place that assumed that crazy behaviour was normal, that madness was logical. Part of me knew that Shirley was having to tread carefully, but why wasn't she reminding him that she had agreed to come for a few weeks, at his specific request after Mum had learned she was to have her kidney removed, that she had a home of her own and a husband waiting for her? Why didn't she tell him how hard it had been to raise the money for the fare? I realised how different my sister was from me, how kind and forbearing. I knew I would have shouted that he was being unfair to me, and to hell with the inevitable good hiding.

That evening Shirley prepared the meal; I helped and we laughed and joked in the warm aroma of sausages and onions. Dad took his and Mum's upstairs, and Shirley and I sat in the kitchen eating while she told me more about America. There was so much I was thirsty to know. Roger had rushed in from work an hour before, and washed, changed and eaten in fifteen minutes flat before tearing out the door again.

After the meal I began to wash up, daydreaming as I plunged a glass into the soap suds, filling it with milky coloured water with froth on the top. I held the glass up to the light and pretended I was the Duchess of Windsor at a party, holding a cocktail. I had just read *The Heart has its Reasons*, her autobiography, and thought she was a glamorous, romantic figure. I couldn't understand why Dad referred to her as 'that American prostitute', but then he was given to that kind of abuse, calling newspapers 'the prostituted press.'

Shirley came into the kitchen, in her coat, breaking my reverie. 'Judy, Billy is asleep, but will you keep an ear open for him, in case he wakes?'

'Of course. Where are you going?'

'Tony and Anne have asked me over for the evening,' and Shirley disappeared upstairs to say goodbye to Mum. I held my breath, counted to ten, and as if on cue, the shouting started. 'What are you going there for? They can come down here to see you. That Judy isn't fit to be left with a baby. What does she know about babies? I don't trust the little cow further than I can see her. She's been nothing but trouble since the day she was born. What are you going to say that can't be said in this house?' I knew Mum would be gripping the dark pink counterpane, its silkiness trapped between her taut fingers, with its matching eiderdown slithering off the bed as if to escape from her agitation.

Shirley said something that I couldn't hear, and then came down the stairs looking strained and tired. 'This house will be the death of me. I'll tell you something, Judy. I'm longing to go home to America. I've been cured of any homesickness for England, that's for sure.'

Then she opened the back door and I heard her heels clicking down the path. Dad came into the kitchen, from the lounge. 'What was all that about?'

'I don't know,' I said, and buried my hands deep in the washing up suds, suddenly intent on scrubbing a pan.

The weekend passed off without further problems, and I was glad to go to school on Monday morning. As the days passed the atmosphere in the house grew tense with Shirley's return to America looming large. Dad had accepted that she would not be staying, but Mum talked as if Shirley would be in England for ever. I marvelled at the bizarreness of it all.

One evening I broached the subject of how the household would cope when Shirley went home.

'You will have to stay at home,' said Dad. 'Someone must be here to look after your mother and run the house. Jill can't because she goes to work.' His tone brooked no discussion and he scarcely looked up from his paper.

I had been expecting this as it was the only logical decision, but my heart sank at the prospect. I was a willing, hard worker and didn't mind what I was asked to do, but the thought of being at home, on my own with Mum and her unpredictable moods, filled me with fear.

I longed to be at school where I could lose myself in the joy of English and History, and the ease of friendship. There I could forget home and its misery, where San Izal, with its stinking, poisonous blackness, slipped to grey as it mixed with hot water.

Chapter 12: Running Away

With Shirley's return to America came a wretched time at Shakespeare Road. There were no light hearted moments, no laughter, simply a blanket of suspicion on Mum's part and defensiveness on Jill's and mine. In retrospect it is clear that Mum's misery and aggression were symptoms of what she would see as further loss of children. She was also being prescribed stronger drugs after the removal of her kidney. It was 1960 and too little was known about her condition. The doctors had believed that removing the suspect kidney would lower her dangerously high blood pressure. It did not, but the drugs must have affected her adversely. Dad asked the doctors not to tell Mum the true state of her health. He kept the seriousness of her situation from her, and convinced Mum that she was slowly getting better. Indeed, Dad told no one, not even Tony, just how ill she was, but bore the burden alone, which meant that all the children believed Mum was regaining her health.

Mum spent most of her time in bed but she was still able to find the strength to struggle down the stairs and make us re-do our household cleaning. Each day we hoped it would be different, although gradually we lost our optimism and hope and became resigned, accepting that this is what our life was.

However, I was changing. I defied the precept that nothing went out the front door, and began to talk to my friend, Val Goodyear whose discretion I trusted. She was not a gossip and her family had always welcomed me. Her mother had once mended my ripped school panama hat when I hadn't dared take it home, without asking any awkward questions about why I was afraid to face my mother.

Now I needed to talk to a friend, someone who would be matter of fact about the whole situation, and who wouldn't make embarrassing comments, who would adopt the same unemotional stance as me. So I told her what went on in our house, wondering if she would believe me. To my surprise, Valt nodded. Then she reminded me of when she had come to call for me one Saturday afternoon. I had opened the door and called, 'Mum, Val's here for me. I've washed the hall floor, can I go out now, please?'

Mum came up the hall with a bucket of dirty water. She swilled it over the floor and said, 'Then you'll have to do it again, won't you?'

I had tried to forget the incident but now it came flooding back. Val said, 'I went away as fast as I could. But the funny thing was that neither of us mentioned it on the following Monday morning, at school. I didn't even tell my mother.'

I had several weeks at home after Shirley returned to America, and then I was allowed to go back to school, part-time, going in halfway through the morning after everything had been done at home, and Mum was comfortable.

Increasingly, Mum's deep dislike for Jill and me increased yet further, and nothing we did or said was right. Dad was never home for the worst excesses, when she would erupt in fury and lash out with anything to hand. I was often sent to the local hardware shop to buy a length of cane for her to use as a weapon. She broke so many, lashing out at us in fury, that the shop ran out.

When Dad came home she would tell him tales that often bore no resemblance to the truth, but he seemed to believe her and we would get another good hiding from him.

Mum was right about my cheek, though. It seemed my only form of self defence and I unwisely used it liberally and in anger. I made every situation worse. Mum had a contempt for my A level studies, and said that I used words she didn't understand. I often wondered why she kept me at school. Then I overheard a conversation between her and Dad, when they decided that I was more use as a schoolgirl. When necessary I could be kept at home, and Dad received a tax allowance for me while I was still in full-time education.

Jill had left school at the age of fifteen and had gone to work. In her last academic year she had been made head girl. She ran home from school to break the news, and Dad said, 'You're head girl? God help the bottom one.' The remark was unintentionally cruel and thoughtless, and his standard reply to success. He thought it was funny. Years later I learned that he boasted about his children's achievements to other people.

Mum was getting better physically but her moods did not improve. I felt permanently tense and watchful, while Jill looked pale, thin and anxious.

One Saturday lunchtime the situation exploded. All morning we had been cleaning, then after Mum had pulled furniture out in a desperate search for dust, we had cleaned again. I had washed the kitchen floor twice and still Mum said that it was dirty. Bleach from scrubbing the lavatory burnt my hands, but she said the pan didn't shine enough.

Mum started to write a shopping list for Luton. We didn't know which of us she would send, or whether we would be allowed to wash and tidy ourselves first. Jill and I exchanged worried glances which Mum noticed.

'Don't you dare look at each other like that. Jill, get your coat on to go to Luton,' and jabbing a vicious finger she said to me, 'you can start washing the paintwork in the bedrooms.'

'Can we have something to eat, first? We haven't had any breakfast.'

At that moment my stomach rumbled and Jill and I laughed.

Mum did not find it funny, and when we persisted in asking for food, she rang Dad at work, to ask him to come home. We knew that Dad would be furious; he hated to receive phone calls when he was working and his anger would be directed against us.

Mum put down the telephone. 'Your father is on his way home now. God help you.'

Jill gripped my arm. 'We can't wait here for him to come home, Judy. Not another good hiding.' Her face was blotched, her eye twitched with tiredness, and she twisted the apron she wore into a tight sausage.

'You're right.' I made an instant decision. 'We'll go to Tony's house. He'll know what to do.' And within seconds we were sprinting up the road, Mum shrieking after us from the doorway, 'You won't get away with this.'

Tony listened to us in silence, and his face grew increasingly grim. In his kitchen we poured out our tale of misery and madness. Finally he said, 'Anne will make sure you have something to eat and drink. I'm going to phone Ro Lee.' This was his friend, a newly appointed circuit judge.

When Tony came back to the kitchen he said, 'Ro says no one can force you to go home as long as I undertake to be your guardian. Unless Mum and Dad fight it legally, that can be an informal arrangement. Now I'm going down to Shakespeare Road to talk to Mum and Dad.'

When Tony came back two hours later he looked shaken. We were waiting anxiously despite Anne's kindness and reassurance. Tony eased his tie from his neck and said, 'Anne, I think she's finally flipped. I couldn't begin to have a sane conversation with her.'

'What did Dad say?' I dared to ask.

'He wasn't there. He'd been home and gone out again. I expect he'll turn up here soon.' Tony sighed, and I wondered if he was regretting our arrival.

A little later as I made a pot of tea, a face appeared at the back door. It was Dad, and my legs began to tremble.

Tony came into the kitchen and was his usual courteous self. 'Hello, Dad. I'm glad you're here. A cup of tea or something stronger?'

'Keep your tea, and your fancy drinks. I've come to take the girls home.' Although he spoke strongly Dad had the look of a beaten man. Still dressed in his working clothes, his face was shadowed and gaunt. And he was angry. 'They come here with their stories and you listen. Only rats desert a sinking ship. Their mother is a sick woman and deserves respect, not the bloody cheek and rudeness she gets from these two.'

Tony spoke quietly. 'Dad, you're putting your head in the sand. If you don't do something she'll end up killing them.'

Suddenly it was all too much. I put my forehead against the cool of the fridge, and sobbed my heart out.

Tony said, 'It's going to be all right, Jude.'

Dad looked at the three of us in turn, an even considered look. 'Judy will wake in the night and know she's done wrong, for she's *my* daughter. Come on, Judy, we're going home.' He turned to Tony. 'You can keep Jill.'

Like a small child I used my fists to rub the tears away, and then silently I followed him out of the door. I was torn. I dreaded going back home, but Dad was right. The guilt would eat at me like canker if I stayed with Tony. There could be no happy resolution.

On the following Monday I drafted a letter to Tony which I didn't send. I decided it was too sanctimonious but didn't know how else to phrase it. In it I tried to thank him for all he had done for me and said that I thought it was my duty to stay at Shakespeare Road. The word 'duty' jarred, and for the first time for a long while I was able to laugh at myself. Then I made the fatal mistake of hiding the letter in my bedroom instead of getting rid of it in some convenient bin away from Shakespeare Road.

On Tuesday evening I washed up and tidied the kitchen, and was just about to get out my homework when Mum said, 'You needn't think you're going to bury your head in those books. There's the ironing to do; you'll have extra jobs now Jill's gone. So get on with it. *That's* your duty.'

I froze, and cursed myself for not getting rid of the letter. Dad frowned at Mum. They had obviously discussed the results of her snooping, and Dad would have come out with one of his usual phrases. 'Don't say anything. Give her enough rope and she'll hang herself.'

Mum was right. There were more jobs now Jill had gone, and more irrational behaviour too. At Christmas she gave me a watch. It was the first one I had ever owned, and had a red leather strap. I put it away carefully until I had finished the housework, as I didn't want bleach or San Izal to corrode it. On Boxing Day Mum took it back, saying I was too cheeky to be given presents. I sat on my bed and cried. That watch, with its beautiful, soft, vivid strap, was symbolic of kindness and warmth. When Mum had stood in the jewellers and chosen it, surely she had been feeling goodwill towards me? If so, she now regretted her kind act.

I met Jill briefly every Saturday morning, while I was doing grocery shopping in Luton. 'I told Tony that you weren't being given your dinner money,' she said. 'He wants you to meet him outside the café in Bute Street on Monday at 12:30.'

I stood patiently outside the steamed up windows for half an hour before Tony arrived. He was never punctual. Jumping out of the car he cried, 'Jude, sorry, usual pressure of work. Let's get inside and order.'

Tony opened the door for me, and I saw his eyes travel down to my feet. But it was not until we had ordered sausages and mash that he said, 'I know I don't know much about sixteen-year-old girls, but are wellington boots the latest fashion, especially when it's fine?'

I tried to sound casual and give my mother's little laugh. 'The other girls wear stockings, but Mum won't buy me any. She says I'm a schoolgirl and mustn't give myself airs and graces. I'm daft enough to shout,' "Why must I be different from everyone else in the sixth form?"

And then of course she bashes me and tells me that I've made her ill again, and just wait until Dad comes home.'

Tony's lips tightened but he only asked quietly, 'What do you wear then?'

'Oh, I've got ankle socks, so I wear my boots to school and then put my plimsolls on as if I've got PE that morning. Everyone wears socks with their plimsolls, for PE, and they often don't bother to change after the lesson. So there's no problem Tony, honestly.'

He smiled at the approaching waiter and said, 'That looks lovely. Thank you,' and made no further comment until we had both started eating. 'I'll give you the money to buy stockings,' he said, 'and you only had to ask.'

'I can't take it. She'd ask me where I'd got the money from, and go mad when I told her. You know she doesn't *know* I meet you, but I think she guesses.'

'Hide the money and hide the stockings.'

'She'd find them. Nothing is secret in that house, not even my thoughts. She's got a sixth sense. What she doesn't know, she makes up. And when I'm at school she goes through my things.'

Tony paused, fork half way to his mouth. 'Jude, I worry about you. You don't even seem to have the basic necessities. How do you cope at school?'

'That's easy. People like Val Goodyear would never laugh at me, and as for the rest'...I shrugged. 'I get in first. I put myself down before they can. They don't know what to say and just move away. As for clothes...we don't wear uniform in the sixth form. I've got a skirt and a couple of jumpers, so I manage to look vaguely respectable.'

'You always seem so cheerful. How do you manage it?'

'Look, what's the point of being anything else? Please stop this, I'm perfectly happy.'

For a while we ate in silence, then Tony said, 'I insist on giving you dinner money. How will you hide that?'

'That's easy. I'll buy the dinner tickets this afternoon and put them in my socks.'

One bleak Sunday in February, three months after Jill had left home, the 6 am summons came. I had slept well despite the dreams which nightly forced their way to a layer just below consciousness, so that I was aware of the disturbed feelings without being able to grasp their substance. At sixteen I still sleep walked occasionally, but as I knew nothing of it except what I was told, that didn't worry me.

'Judy!' I had lingered in my bed a little too long. I struggled out of the cocoon of blankets, and curled my toes back in self defence as they touched the icy lino. Stumbling across the floor I went to switch on the light before remembering that it had been removed for punishment. To be sent to bed early without the luxury of being able to read was a terrible sanction for me, and unwisely I had let Mum know. What my crime was this time I don't remember, but usually it was answering back.

The light on the landing guided me downstairs. That light was always on because Mum was frightened of the dark. I went into the kitchen with its pervasive smell of San Izal and made the tea, shivering in my nightdress and bare feet, and carried the cups upstairs to my parents. I put my father's cup down first: 'Dad, your tea!'

He opened one eye, mumbled 'Piss,' and went back to sleep again. No one could make a cup as strong as he liked it. His stomach lining must have resembled tanned leather.

Then round to my mother's side of the bed where I carefully put her tea down. 'I hope you rinsed my cup under a boiling kettle before you poured out my tea!'

'Yes, Mum. I always do.'

'Don't 'yes Mum' me. You're as cunning as a wagon load of monkeys, a born liar. Get some clothes on and get on with the kitchen floor. I'll be down in a bit to inspect it. Make sure you clean in the corners thoroughly.' That was a usual comment from Mum, whose maxim was, 'Take care of the corners and the middle will take care of itself.'

As I crawled over the floor, regularly wringing out the cloth in the scalding liquid I mentally scratched the fears uppermost in my mind. The next day was medical day at school, and I wanted a bath before facing the doctor and nurse. It was bad enough having to strip with a slowly developing figure: how I wished I could retain the flatness which had been mine for so long. I could do nothing about that but at least could turn up spotlessly clean. The obstacle was Mum. If she was in a reasonable mood, and if I stayed 'in favour' then she might agree to let me turn on the electric immersion heater for a bath. But if I offended, then I could forget it. There was also the gym display. I belonged to gym club and the next afternoon after school we were to give a display. I was unsure if Mum would give me permission to stay, and I dreaded having to make excuses to the PE teacher, of whom I was afraid.

When I heard Mum's tread on the stairs I felt tense and sick, and I watched warily as she poked around in the corners. But the kitchen passed its close inspection, probably because I did not have to go to school, and because Dad was still in the house.

'I suppose it just passes muster,' said Mum, 'You can make yourself tea and a slice of toast before going upstairs to start on the bedrooms.'

By this time my father had coughed and choked his way out of bed, drunk some more 'piss' and had his first rollup of the day. Then he had made his way to his Sunday part time job, serving petrol, closely followed out of the house by Roger, who also earned himself a few extra pounds at the petrol pumps.

I sat on my bed, my feet tucked under me to protect them from the cold. In my memory it is always cold at Shakespeare Road, and my ex-husband agreed. He used to keep our central heating at a steady 20 degrees, and when I attempted to turn it up would say, 'How anyone brought up at Shakespeare Road can complain of the cold, beats me.' The first thing my son does when he visits me is turn down the heating, saying, 'This house is far too hot,' but I intend never to be cold again.

I sat on the bed listening to my mother chatting to my young sister downstairs, and worried about the bath situation and the medical, and the gym display. Finally I went to the top of the stairs and called, 'Mum!'

'Don't shout like that. Have you finished the bedrooms yet? You can't possibly have done them properly in that time!'

'Mum, I haven't done anything yet. Mum can I put the bathroom immersion on so that I can have a bath later? I've got a medical tomorrow.'

'What do you mean you haven't started the bedrooms yet? What have you been doing all this time? You idle little cow. Don't talk to me about baths ~ get on with that bloody work'

The morning went from bad to worse. I became defiant and rude, and Mum gave my dinner to the dog. I felt I had nothing to lose. But panic was beginning to rise in me, and as I washed the cream paintwork either side of the stair runner, I tried again in desperation. 'Mum, can I put the immersion on please?'

She was furious. As she shouted out my crimes, real and imaginary, a buzzing sound filled my ears and suddenly everything became enveloped in a mist.

'I hate you woman, I hate you. I wish you were dead.' And I kicked over the bucket of San Izal, wrenched open the front door, and ran down the path.

It had been raining earlier that day, and the cotoneaster hedge bordering the front of our garden was dripping rhythmically, arched over the small wall. My sleeve caught on one of its twigs and a shower of drops poured down my arm. It seemed appropriate and I didn't care that my arm was soaking wet.

I had no money for bus fare so I half walked, half ran the couple of miles to Tony and Anne's house, blurted out a story about needing a bath for a medical and not knowing if Mum would let me. I made a ridiculous figure but they didn't laugh, and Anne suggested I had my bath before a hot meal. Standing in their shower, with the hot stream of water ridding me of the smell of San Izal and the ache of unhappiness, I felt a rare contentment. I wouldn't let myself think about what would happen when I went home again, or the certain good hiding I'd get from Dad.

Over lunch I related what had been going on at home. I tried to make it funny and Anne and Jill were soon laughing. Tony was very quiet and seemed lost in thought. I was aware that he was looking at me and felt uncomfortable. Finally he spoke. 'I think it's time you came to live here, Judy. The situation is becoming ridiculous.'

'I agree,' said Anne.

I struggled with my thoughts. Part of me longed to join this household, run by Anne with quiet efficiency, a home full of sense, humour and civilised attitudes. Jill already lived there and it would be good to be with my sister again. But how would they manage without me at Shakespeare Road? I didn't think I'd be missed for myself, but I wondered who would do the housework if I went.

I looked up to find Tony still watching me. As if he could read my thoughts he said, 'They'll cope, Jude. Her antagonism towards you cannot be healthy for either of you. God knows what she'll do if you stay there much longer.'

I felt a sense of relief that my leaving Shakespeare Road might actually benefit my mother, and this was inextricably mixed with a sense of desolation at her hatred of me. Suddenly I felt an overwhelming weariness. I could not continue the daily struggle for much longer, although, at sixteen, the years at home seemed to stretch ahead interminably. I looked first at Tony, then at Anne. 'Thank you,' I said.

I went back to Shakespeare Road that evening to collect my school books, clothes and possessions. Everything I had fitted into my satchel and a carrier bag. I crept in through the back door, expecting the living room door to fly open and an irate parent to confront me.

But they remained absorbed by the television, and if they heard me, must have thought that I had gone to bed. There would be plenty of time the next morning for retribution. I didn't risk going downstairs again, however, but climbed out of my bedroom window, ran down the back garden, and out to the road through an alley. Tony was at the top of the road in his car, waiting. He took me back to his house, then drove back to tell my parents that I was moving in with him.

It was, by his own admission, one of the hardest things he ever had to do. The next day Jill told me that she overheard Anne and Tony talking about it. It was midnight before he came back, emotionally exhausted. It appeared Mum had screamed and shouted, and then practically collapsed. Dad had shown a cold, white fury, and spoken of rats and sinking ships, and how Tony had destroyed the family.

'Have I done the right thing, Anne? Should I take Judy back there?'

But Anne was adamant. 'Look, Tony, I've never been part of the Darby madness. I can stand back and look at it objectively. You can't send Judy back to that house. They'll destroy her.'

'I know you're right. But I never want to face what I've had to face tonight, ever again.'

I never spoke to my mother again. I only saw her twice. Once I was with Jill and we came face to face with her in Dunstable High Street. We came upon her suddenly. I suspect that I would have run if I had seen her in time. The situation was uncanny. Mum addressed the whole of her conversation to Jill and ignored me totally, so much so that I started to believe I was invisible. I was wearing a big, baggy cardigan, a style popular with the sixth form, that Anne had helped me to knit. When Jill saw Mum again, the one comment made about me, was, 'I didn't like Judy's cardigan.'

The other time I saw Mum was in Luton town shopping centre. She didn't see me, and I was able to get a clear look at her. She seemed old, gaunt and wretched, and it was hard to believe she was only forty-nine. I wanted to run up to her and ask if there was anything I could do. I stifled the urge, knowing how it would be received.

By leaving home I had stepped over a line that meant I could not be forgiven. I had done my part in destroying the bundle of sticks. Yet Jill was welcomed on her visits. Tony had not allowed me to go to Shakespeare Road once I had left. He simply said that it was not a good idea. So perhaps Mum and Dad believed I wanted to separate myself from them completely.

Tony said that I was to pass my A levels, go away to higher education, and when I was qualified he was certain my parents would welcome me again with pride, as a success story. With new status, I would be treated totally differently.

It was not to be.

One Thursday evening after school, nine months later, I jumped off the bus in Dunstable. Usually, I walked home alone from there, but that Thursday I found Tony and Jill parked, waiting for me.

'Jude, Mum died an hour ago.'

I climbed in the back of the car, stunned, with nothing to say. The grey November evening suddenly seemed threatening and unreal. As if on cue, the clouds broke, and I watched the pavement fill with raindrops, like painting by numbers.

Behind lighted windows people went about familiar tasks, mundane and satisfying. What had happened to the normality of my Thursday evening? Why wasn't I running up Garden Road, satchel swinging, turning into Hawthorn Close, thinking about my History homework, the delicious meal Anne would have cooked, reading *Peter Rabbit* to my nephew, Gregory, before he went to sleep? Ordinary, enjoyable things, to be savoured and cherished.

Tony started the car and drove through Dunstable High Street, quiet now that the shops had closed, down Church Street, past Bagshawe's where Dad worked, past 322 Luton Road where it had all begun, and down Shakespeare Road. We travelled the whole way in silence, and I was reminded of the day we had made a similar silent journey the morning after Roy died.

We drew up outside the cotoneaster hedge, rain still dripping from it, misery incarnate; the brass strip on the doorstep still shining bravely in defiance; the gate catch still providing opposition.

The smell of San Izal hit me forcibly as we walked through the back door, and I gasped. It was as if I had never been away. In the front room my father sat hunched over the fire, prematurely defeated and old. As I stood uncertainly in the doorway he glanced up, and his eyes met mine with that penetrating look so well remembered, assessing, shrewd, but now with something else lurking also. It frightened me, it made me ashamed. I dared not analyse what that might be.

His voice was weary: 'Come in, Judy, there's no need to be afraid.'

'I'm not afraid, Dad.' The spark was expected of me, I knew that, but it took a superhuman effort to summon it.

The centre light was on, stark and revealing, shade at a crooked angle as if disturbed. The room was warm, stiflingly so, at odds with the rest of that freezing house, but Dad eased even closer to the fire as if for comfort.

He gazed into the fire, and for a moment it seemed as if we would all remain for evermore in that uncomfortable silence. Then he straightened up and began to talk so quietly that I had to strain my ears to hear. He explained what he had probably recounted already that evening. 'She collapsed while eating her tea. She was laughing and talking one minute, then she suddenly slumped and fell forward. I had cooked her meal.'

Dad gestured helplessly. 'It was bacon and egg, she enjoyed that. I gave it to her on a tray, in front of the fire, in that chair there.' He looked hard at the chair as if he could still see Mum. 'I phoned Dr. Ashton, and he had already called an ambulance before he came. They took her to hospital, but she was dead before they got there.' He paused in disbelief. 'And the hospital only round the corner. They let me see her, and I kissed her goodbye, and started to leave. They tried to call me back, said did I want someone to talk to, did I want a cup of tea? I told them to fuck off and came home.'

His face suddenly dissolved, and silent slow tears eased themselves down his face. I stood there, still just inside the door, drinking in his terrible grief, picturing this proud, vulnerable man striding away from the hospital. I could not look at him. My eyes travelled to the sideboard and there lay the red strapped watch that had been mine for one day. Dad followed my gaze.

'Your mother said you have a birthday soon, your eighteenth, she said. She was going to send you your watch.'

The fire hissed, a hot white coal fell on to the hearth. We all focused our attention on it in silence, and then my father leaned forward and picked it up with his coarse, leathery fingers to throw back in the fire. 'It's made a mess,' he said. 'She wouldn't have liked that. She liked things to be nice.'

Mum was buried five days later, on my birthday. Somehow, that seemed appropriate.

Chapter 13: Breaking Point

For a time after my mother's death I inhabited my own world of punishment and recrimination. The experience was terrifying and I began to dread the dark as keenly as had my mother while she was alive. At that thought I froze: was she *still* afraid of the dark?

I thought back to Roy's funeral. I thought of him nailed down against his will, fighting for breath, dying in an agony of suffocation.

In the years before he died my father was felt that the ghosts surrounding him at Shakespeare Road were friendly. In that house my grandmother had died in bed; downstairs my mother had collapsed and died in front of a comforting November fire; on a grim October day Roy had died a few hundred yards away: if he had been able to drag himself to a window the lights of home would have beckoned him. In Dad's thoughts, these were harmonious ghosts.

I could find no such solace for I knew my parents had considered me treacherous for running away. My father's pitiless words that day in Tony's kitchen constantly ran through my head:

*This is **my** daughter: she will wake in the night and know she has done wrong.*

And in those days following my mother's death, I did wake in the night, every night, and felt guilt pressing the life from me, until like my brother, like my mother, I could breathe no longer. The brief months of warmth, laughter, welcoming friends to Tony's home, being allowed to go visiting or to the pictures, the delight in my studies, were at an end. Simple daily pastimes which had given me joy, now were burnt out cinders, and I wondered about the girl who had experienced such pleasure in life. Was I imagining her? Had she existed?

Sometimes I dreamed that my mother was still alive, that she was calling me to wake up and make her a cup of tea. She would be smiling, happy, telling me that I was a good girl, that I always did as I was told. Then I would awake and feel the silence of the house, with the blackness encompassing me in a merciless stranglehold, and I would despair.

At this time I became evermore gregarious, avoiding my own company, throwing myself into anything that was going on. With sudden clarity I understood my mother's fear of being alone in the house. What had been her emotions, had she been suffering from guilt, also? Is that why she craved company and attention, an affirmation that she was liked and accepted?

I had a new recklessness. I spoke without thinking. My English school report was written by a perceptive teacher. After generous comment on my appreciation of literature she wrote: *...but at times Judith makes comments, not only disconcerting to others, but also to herself.* Tony took his responsibilities as my guardian very seriously, and was furious. 'Are you the classroom clown, or the self appointed arbiter of the truth?' I said nothing.

I realised that I couldn't continue in this way; something inside gnawed away at me. One of Mum's insults was to refer to me as 'the little actress with big, thick lips, and a mouth like a gash.' and after her death 'the little actress' played a part. No one in the family asked me what I felt; I asked no one how *they* felt. It wasn't the Darby way. Therefore, I could act as if all was well while I was with others and while the light was on.

On the morning of Mum's funeral I went into Dunstable town centre with Anne and my cousin, Norman, who had come from Ebbw Vale to represent my Uncle Wally, Dad's brother. Norman had taken us in his car to buy a few last items of food for the guests who would return to Shakespeare Road after the funeral. Anne disappeared into a bakery, and in the middle of the high street Norman turned to me: 'Judy, you look awful.'

I dragged myself upwards to meet the occasion, laughing. 'Do you always insult your cousins? Is it a Welsh custom?'

'You know I wasn't insulting you, Judy. You're my lovely young cousin; I just wish I could make today a little easier for you all.'

'You're here, supporting us, Norman, and that means a lot.' Then suddenly, I burst out, 'Norman, it's my birthday today, and a birthday has never felt quite as strange as this.'

He looked shocked, and immediately thrust his hand in his pocket, drawing out a five pound note.

'Oh, Judy, even 'happy birthday' is inappropriate, but please take this and...and afterwards buy yourself some of those history books you love.'

By now I was shrivelling with embarrassment and cursing my spontaneity.

'No, Norman, I don't want it, but thank you for the thought. I shouldn't have said anything. Mum always says I speak out of turn...'

I broke off and we stood looking at each other, relieved when Anne interrupted us with her cheerful, 'Well, that's everything now. Let's go home and get the rest of the rolls filled.'

I remember little of the rest of the day. I remember sitting in the funeral car, with the rest of the family, and Tony saying quietly to Dad, 'You wouldn't have wanted her to go after you, and have had to face this. We can be grateful for that,' and Dad nodded and then retreated to his impenetrable world.

That evening, back at Tony and Anne's home, we waved off Norman. I then said that I had an essay to write, and would go up to my bedroom.

Just a minute, Jude.'

I paused at the door.

'This is your day, too. I'm afraid we all forgot.'

Squirming inside, I muttered, 'Natural , considering...'

'We wouldn't have chosen today, Dad and me, if we'd realised.'

'Tony, it doesn't matter. And how do you think I'd have felt if you'd changed the day because of me?'

I wanted to say, 'I feel bad enough,' but the words wouldn't come. I was also conscious that Tony looked haggard and if he was sharing his thoughts, it wasn't with me.

I started to leave. 'Jude, Anne thought you might like a birthday cake, but I didn't think so.

'You're right.'

'You know you keep saying you'd love to go up to London, to Foyles' second hand history department? Well, go in a couple of weeks and we'll pay the fare and give you some money to buy books. Oh, and Norman left you some money, too.'

I stumbled through my thanks and turned once more for the door.

'What's the haste? One more thing: Dad told me to give you this watch. Mum was going to give you it back on your birthday.'

For a few months after Mum's death, I continued to live with Tony and Anne.

For several weeks Tony went to Shakespeare Road late every night and sat talking to Dad about politics, horse racing, books, anything but Mum. Tony was worried that Dad might end it all, as he had become withdrawn and morose, with interest in nothing.

Shirley wrote to Dad, asking him for something small of Mum's as a memento, and received a terse reply:

Why should I send something to the daughter who went away to America and broke her mother's heart?

I knew that I could not carry on the way I was going, heading for a breakdown. For the most part I acted out my life: it was as if I was sitting on my own shoulder watching myself with dislike and contempt. Sometimes I went several days without eating, withholding food from myself where once I had railed against my mother withholding it from me for punishment. Hunger made me feel purged, somehow cleaner. It was a precursor of the anorexia nervosa I was to suffer from some years later.

In this mood of self flagellation, studying A Level literature didn't help, least of all Macbeth:
> *Sleep in the affliction of these terrible dreams*
> *that shake us nightly...*
> *...Better be with the dead,*
> *whom we, to gain our peace, have sent to peace.*

Then, weeks later, I woke up one morning, feeling nothing. It was weird, but it meant I could enjoy life again, at least superficially. All the suffering had disappeared overnight. I grinned wryly to myself and at myself, as Milton came to mind: *Calm of mind, all passion spent,* not realising that this new-found peace would be paid for with a massive breakdown four years later.

After Mum's death Jill had returned to Shakespeare Road, but after a few weeks had come back to Tony's again, as she and her father had clashed. His grief, still raw, had found a scapegoat in Jill. After returning to Tony's house she began to save to go to live in America, to be with Shirley.

By then I felt strong and invincible. 'I'm going back to Shakespeare Road, Tony. I think Dad would like some help. I'll be quite useful . I'm good at housework.'

'And what about your exams, our dream of you going to university?'

'I can still study. It won't make any difference.'

'Do what you want.' Tony's voice was icy, and for the first time for a very long while, I found myself sobbing.

'Tony, please don't be angry. I couldn't bear it, especially after you've done so much for me.'

'I'm thinking of you. You've made so much progress since you came here, and I'm afraid you're throwing your chances away. I hope this isn't some dramatic, martyred gesture.'

I went back to Shakespeare Road the following Saturday, and stayed.

Judy - 1962 aged 18

At Shakespeare Road it was as if my mother was still there. Her fur coat, bought for Tony's wedding, hung carelessly over the bannister in the hall. Two pairs of her shoes stood neatly near the front door. Upstairs, an orange dress, a favourite of hers, drooped over a landing chair. Her bedroom was as if she might walk in any moment, with her clothes in the wardrobe and her make-up and perfume cluttering the dressing table. The drawers were also as she had left them, crammed full of discarded tablets, syringes and ampoules.

I now shared this room with my younger sister. Dad slept in the third bedroom, the smallest. One morning in the Easter school holiday, I called to my father as he raced out of the door to work. 'Dad, I'm going to clear out Mum's things today.'

He said nothing, giving tacit consent. Then, he came back two minutes later.

'Not her fur coat; I want Anne to take that to Shirley. Tony says she is going to visit her soon.'

I started with the hall, putting the shoes in a large cardboard box. Moving upstairs, the orange dress joined the shoes. I then took a deep breath and started on the bedroom, sweeping creams, lipsticks, powder and perfume from the dressing table into the box. At the bottom of the wardrobe I found the adoption papers and some letters from Mum to Dad when we lived in Felpham, and he was making the weekly journey from Sussex to Bedfordshire. I was five. In one letter Mum wrote:

Judy lost her shoes playing on the beach. She cannot go to school until I can afford some more. That child will be the death of me.

I struggled down the garden with the full box of my mother's clothes and personal possessions. Lighting the bonfire, I stood back and watched her life going up in flames. When Dad came home he gave no greeting, but walked down the garden to where drifts of smoke were still visible. Coming back to the kitchen, he said, 'You made the bonfire on the rhubarb patch. That means we won't get any this year.'

Anne took the fur coat to Missouri when she visited Shirley a few months later. Already there were murmurings afoot about the morality of wearing real fur, and she found hauling the cumbersome garment on and off the aeroplane embarrassing and cumbersome. It was too big to go in a suitcase.

Shirley was no less embarrassed by the gift, but accepted it for what it clearly was, a peace-offering from Dad for his vitriol when she had requested a memento.

She never wore the coat but gave it to her small children to play with, and it became a bear.

Tony felt vindicated when I didn't do well in my A levels. In the examination room I felt detached from the whole process, and spent the first half hour of each exam gazing, without interest, at the paper. I passed all three but not well enough for university entrance. In 1962 the competition was fierce, the requirements great. However, I was pleased with my distinction on the Shakespeare paper. As well as Macbeth we had studied Henry IV Part 2, and as I wrote about Hal's treatment of Falstaff: *I know thee not, old man, fall to your prayers,* I felt tears in my eyes for the rejected. Even then, I did not realise how emotionally fragile I had become.

I went to teacher training college, and allowed an elderly, very correct teacher to choose it for me. I had no interest in what happened to me. It was Church of England, single sex, with May Day celebrations and annual election of a May Queen. I hated my years there, despite making some good friends. Going home for the holidays I felt I had no place there, either. I felt invisible. I was unaware that my father, now more cheerful and settled, had noticed. He wrote to Shirley:

Judy came home for the holiday, but of late I detect something amiss. She seems to be moody and overloaded with worry. I suspect that her non conformist political views at the college may be getting her into hot water. She would have done better at university where her views would be welcomed, but this college seems more like a young ladies' seminary. True blue and all that. I do not know what she will do after leaving this summer, I don't suppose she knows herself. I offer no advice in this respect, it would be useless to attempt it.

Dad was not entirely wrong. We had a mock election at the college for the 1965 General Election, and I stood as the Labour candidate. It did not go down well with the authorities, who were prepared to be benign until they saw the support I was getting. Even my History lecturer told me that she was amused but felt I wasn't being wise. I didn't win, the students' background prevented them from voting for the unthinkable.

Val Goodyear went off to Leicester, and had a wonderful time at that progressive, mixed college. Many times over the three years I wished I had done likewise.

But it wasn't just college which depressed me. The world seemed a cold, bleak place with no joy. If anyone had asked what had ailed me I couldn't have explained for I didn't know. The decision about my future was made for me: my grammar school wrote to offer me a teaching post, and I accepted, taking the easy way out.

Before that could happen I had to take my final exams at college. I sat through each exam motionless, the paper as pristine as when I began. I ended up in a mental hospital, and my willingness to do so, albeit reluctantly, caused a rift between Tony and me that was to last for three years, before our old closeness reasserted itself. He had felt that I should battle on without professional help, and also that nothing should be revealed to any psychiatrist. When I followed this precept I was given primitive ECT which left me confused and with partial temporary amnesia. Tony was so angry with me for accepting medical assistance that he even stayed away from my wedding, and his rejection bit deeply.

Without the support of Tony, my best friend, my recovery was slow and painful, and recovery is perhaps the wrong word. Instead I managed to make a pact with life, that I would function normally as far as the world was concerned as long as my emotions could be suppressed, allowing me to numb the pain, the guilt and longing for acceptance.

I accepted the first and only man who asked to marry me, and settled down to my career, obsessive studying, marriage and motherhood, my life apparently mapped out for me.

Dad had just celebrated his sixty-seventh birthday when he died of lung cancer in 1972. He had not had long to enjoy retirement, but Tony occasionally took him on holiday with his young family. He also took him to race meetings such as Epsom and Goodwood, making sure Dad had a good time, wining and dining him well.

But Tony came to dread the journeys home and Dad's uncharacteristic, emotional revelations. As the car purred through the dark lanes Dad would become deeply depressed, the drink loosening his tongue and emotions, and say that there were certain of his children he couldn't look in the eye.

Tony's response was always cryptic: 'Your children understand, Dad.'

I hope we do.

Chapter 14: Aftermath

I had recovered but I never stopped thinking about my adopted sister, Judy, even though, once I had left school there were no more glimpses of her in the corridor. A few days before I went away to college my History teacher invited me to spend the evening with her and her husband. During the evening she talked about her plans for the year. She handed me the list of LVI names. 'I thought you might like to see which girls are going to do A Level History this year.'

Casually I glanced down the list. One name jumped out at me: *Judy Woods.* She was also on the English list: my adopted sister shared my interests. Later I learned that Judy also went on to qualify as a teacher. I knew nothing else.

Then with the help of my friend, Val Goodyear, a skilled amateur genealogist, I learnt more things about the other Judy's life. In 1989 we went searching through the national birth records, housed then in St. Catherine's House, Holborn, and I received a shock when I discovered that the seventh Darby child had been registered with my name, Judy.

Shortly after reading the entry in the big, heavy, dusty volume in the echoing atmosphere of St. Catherine's, I wrote to Val Goodyear:

I keep seeing that page, in that directory, about Judy Woods. I don't know why, but I feel so strange that someone, almost certainly my father, for whatever reason, put my name down for a child who was not me.

With Val's help I found that that Judy Woods had married and had two sons. She still lived in Bedfordshire. Tony said that we couldn't approach her: it was possible, although unlikely, that she didn't know she was adopted; it was also possible that she knew all about us and didn't want contact. Any approach must be left to the other Judy. I saw the sense of that. After all, I had spent years at school keeping my knowledge secret, terrified of my parents' reaction if they even knew we attended the same school. I was not meant to know of her existence. This was ironic, as every time they had rowed, my mother had shouted, 'You made me give my baby away!'

So there it was left. In 2003, Tony died, Roger died four years later: our family was shrinking rapidly. Then, in September 2007, I came home late one evening, weary from teaching, and found a message from Greg, Tony's son. Bedfordshire Social Services had been in touch with him, trying to trace Jill and me. It was clear that it was not known that Jill had been living in America since she was twenty.

I realised that Judy Woods had decided to find her birth family; I was shaken.

'If you like,' said Greg, 'I'll tell them that Jill has changed her name to Clinton and lives in the White House, and you were last seen disappearing down the Orinoco in a canoe.'

The next day I phoned Social Services. A woman called Carol was very cautious. In her view I could be ignorant of the other Judy's existence. I told her that I knew what this was all about. Suddenly she opened up.

Carol said that the first step would be for me to write to my adopted sister. Carol would approve the letter before delivering it personally. Then Judy would have the opportunity to write to me.

The letter wasn't easy to compose, but I wrote it at speed. Shirley and I had already decided that she should know what we knew. There was much we didn't know and never would. So on that Wednesday afternoon in late September, I sat down and wrote:

Ever since that June evening in 1953, at Dunstable Eisteddfod, when we both won our classes, you have been on the periphery of my life. My (our) eldest sister, Shirley, told me on the way home that you were my sister, but that I must say nothing. I said nothing, but never forgot…

Judy wrote back promptly:
Reading your letter I was overcome with so many different emotions.

I'd never imagined that I would be known to my birth family…when I eventually read my adoption papers and learned of my origins I thought that my siblings had probably been told that I had died at birth…

…I have put my mobile phone number at the top of this letter as I feel I don't want to waste any more time in moving on to the next stage of my life. I'm really looking forward to meeting you and catching up with a lifetime…

Meeting Judy, in Dunstable, close to where we had both lived unknown to each other, as children, had its own poignancy.

Over several meetings, endless cups of coffee, and various sandwiches and salads, we talked. Conversation was easy: I felt an immediate affinity with this sister I had once observed from a distance. But how do you give an accurate picture of the past, especially to someone with whom you might have shared and lived that past?

I felt that Judy must be receiving a one-sided picture of her parents, especially her father. But how else could it be, when she had to digest the fact that her parents literally gave her away?

I am grateful we have found each other and I cherish our friendship as we try to make sense of the past.

Chapter 15: Meeting

Dunstable on a grey, September morning: once a thriving market town, now a victim of the closure of Vauxhall in nearby Luton, with its boarded up shops and quiet high street. I am early, and I stand there waiting, trembling slightly, racked with emotions and memories. The irony of our meeting place is not lost on me. In this town we had both started life; here we had entered the music festivals and learned not only the joy of winning but also the relief of managing to live up to others' expectations. Here Judy Woods had lived next door to Miss Moss who had taught the rest of the Darby siblings, but had not taught her for she went to a different school, here I had roamed the streets with Roy and fled to the sanctuary of Tony's house when life became too traumatic with my mother, and it was at this very spot that Tony had met me off the bus and broken the news that my mother had suddenly died.

Images that have haunted me all my life return as I await this meeting in Dunstable: the music festival memory, the rare glimpses of Judy Woods at the high school, and then there is the cruellest memory of all. The Friday at school, on an overcast November morning, when I passed my sister in the corridor, and realised that now she would never know the woman who had given birth to her.

The woman I am waiting for emerges from the side road. Judy Woods. I watch her carefully from my vantage point. This shouldn't be me here, it should be Tony or Shirley, who were always wiser than I was. Tony would have the right words. Shirley would be sympathetic. But Tony was dead and Shirley was in Missouri: the moment is mine.

Judy Woods is slim, smart and as attractive as I remember. She is a Darby, with our mother's beautiful eyes echoing the same vulnerability. Her dark hair is also our mother's.

We stand for a brief moment looking at each other. I am hurled back into the past. I am a child again standing in the town hall, looking at another small child, smiling at her, 'What's your name?'

But I am an adult: I lack the confidence and innocence of my young self. I know who she is now; I know the heartbreaking details surrounding her birth. She does not. I know that this meeting is crucial, that I long for this sister to like me. I fear that she may resent her birth family, that however carefully I explain the circumstances she will feel a sense of abandonment. How could she not?

Tentatively, I smile at her. Her smile is warm and genuine in return. We hug awkwardly, and I say, 'Where shall we go for coffee?'

'There is a nice little cafe which belongs to Priory Church just down the high street. Let's go there.'

She is brisk and organised and I am not. I will get to recognise and admire this more and more in the coming weeks and months, and wonder if I would have been like her with a different upbringing. But now I am trying hard to come to terms with the fact that I have finally properly met this sister, am walking down the road with her and making polite conversation, postponing the words which matter until we are seated with the coffee.

I go to order the drinks and realise that I don't know how she drinks her coffee. There is something strange about asking. I should know. She is my sister. She smiles at me as if she understands what I am thinking.

'Black, please, with a small jug of hot water.'

The drinks arrive and she looks at my hot chocolate. 'Don't you like coffee?'

'Yes, but I'm a pleb. I only drink instant. I don't think they serve that here.'

For a moment or two we sit in silence. Then I say, 'Where do you want me to begin, Judy?'

'Anywhere. I have wondered so long about my birth family. I always knew I was adopted but it was never mentioned by my adoptive parents. They didn't know I knew. But a little boy told me in the playground at school. I don't know why but I didn't go home and tell my mother. Something must have told me that they didn't want me to know.'

'What were they like, Judy, your adoptive parents?'

'They were kind; they loved me, they were good to me.'

I feel a tremendous sense of relief and say quietly, 'I'm really glad about that.'

Silence falls again, then I blurt out, 'Our mother didn't want to give you away. It broke her heart.'

Judy says nothing but stirs her coffee reflectively.

I rush on, 'And, although it can't make it any easier for you, there was nothing personal in the decision. It was all decided long before you were born. They must have considered giving me away, too. Dad was growing increasingly desperate about lack of money and mounting debt.'

As our conversation progresses we both begin to relax. We find that we like each other, have interests in common, have a similar sense of humour. We both love literature and History, also music, although she is far more knowledgeable about that than I am.

Judy talks about the fact that there is a sister younger than her.

'I know it's irrational, but to know that another child was kept after giving me away on the grounds they couldn't afford another baby isn't easy to absorb.'

'Emotions aren't rational, and I'd feel exactly the same way, anyone would. But it was because of the terrible grief our mother felt after losing you, that made Dad realise that he couldn't ask it of her again. She cared, Judy, she cared. Not enough was understood in the 1940s about the traumatic effects of giving up a child. She thought she was being punished for giving you away, when Roy died.'

We talk about our own experiences of pregnancy and childbirth, and how grateful we are for our children. When Judy tells me how sick she was in pregnancy, I say, 'You're a true Darby. We all suffered in the same way.'

The time flashes by. We ask a waitress to take our photograph, standing close, smiling, happy to be together. And when we part, it is with reluctance. 'I've found you and I'm not going to lose you,' says Judy.

'I'm not going to let you. You won't escape a second time.'

Epilogue

An adopted sister's story

It was a cold, damp, October day and I was sitting nervously in my car, watching other people passing by, going about their daily lives. I was early for an appointment that I'd waited for all my life and now the day had come, strangely, was in no hurry to keep it.

As I watched everyone passing by, I wondered whether she was early - had she parked her car in the same car park? I'd never met her, perhaps she was one of the women hurrying past, anxious to be out of the drizzle, and warm again.

The time had come. I couldn't wait any longer, so, riddled with nerves, I locked my car and walked towards the unknown. I reached the crossing, looked across the road and there she was, part of the puzzle that I'd been trying to solve all my life, my sister.

It all started when I was four or five years old. I attended a small private school which I hated, mainly because singing and arithmetic had priority over everything else taught there, and I was useless at both. Time after time I was made to stand on a chair, in front of the class, supposedly to enable me to reach the high notes instead of growling away at the bottom. Frequently, play times and story times would see me away from the others trying to get my sums right. I wasn't bothered so much about missing play times as I was often ridiculed by the owner, and only teacher's older son and daughter, but I loved story times. After one particularly miserable playtime, one of them told the other that I'd done something stupid 'because she's adopted.' Funnily, I knew what that word meant because my young cousin was adopted and I knew all about his arrival to my aunt and uncle. However, no one had ever told me that I, too, was a similar case.

Anyone else would probably have gone home and asked their parents after such a revelation, but not me. I must have had a sixth sense that the information wouldn't have been received very well.

Through the years, I often wondered about my birth family and if I saw anyone that I thought resembled me, also wondered whether they were related. Growing up as an only child, I often longed for a sister or brother, particularly when times were hard. I made up various scenarios, imagining perhaps an American GI who'd 'got my mother into trouble' after the war, and who probably didn't even know about me and other similar situations.

Another problem occurred at the High School when I was thirteen and allowed to go on a school trip abroad. Of course I needed a passport, and to acquire a passport you have to have a birth certificate. Surprisingly, my birth certificate had been lost, so off my mother went to see the Headmistress to sort out the problem. Unknown to my mother of course, I knew exactly what was going on, but still remained silent and unquestioning.

A short form certificate was miraculously produced that only showed my name and date of birth, unlike everyone else's which showed names of father and mother and other details. I continued my High school education, sometimes being smiled at by a senior girl who passed me in the corridor. Years later I would find out who she was.

I left school, went to college, became engaged to be married and was invited by another cousin to introduce my fiancé to him and some even more distant cousins that I'd never met. We all met, one Saturday evening in a village pub and I was introduced to one of the distant cousins as 'Dorothy's daughter'. 'Oh yes,' he said, 'you must be the adopted one.' I agreed and no more was said on that subject. Luckily, the only person that I'd ever told about my strange entrance into the world, was my fiancé, so it was no surprise to him.

I married, had two baby boys and eventually Mum and Dad died, not ever knowing that I had known all my life the secret that they had so carefully kept from me.

Why had I never mentioned that I knew? Who knows, I don't – perhaps I didn't want to hurt them. They had given me a secure, happy childhood and had loved me so much. I hadn't betrayed their secret. The only person I'd ever told had been my husband – not even my children or closest friends knew. Also, I'd always felt ashamed that I was adopted and different from everyone else. I'd had years of practice of changing the subject when such issues had been brought up by friends and acquaintances.

Once, on playground duty together with a classroom assistant, I'd had to reprimand a child for behaving badly. 'Oh,' said the assistant, 'he's adopted, all adopted children are strange.' I didn't say anything but it hurt.

Mum died first followed a year later by Dad. I had to clear their house and was anxious to locate an old wooden box which I knew housed private documents to which I'd never been party. This box, which I'd always thought would hold the key to my identity, was not where it had always been kept and couldn't be found anywhere else in the house. I was devastated. At that point, my now adult sons were helping me clear years of rubbish and couldn't understand why I was so upset. I broke down and told them. Two more people now knew my secret. I mistakenly thought that that if I didn't have evidence of my birth name, I would not be able to access my family records. I finally realised that I would never know who I really was. That was a very low point.

A few months later I accompanied a friend to her house in Spain. We had an eventful journey. Our hire car broke down and we eventually arrived at our destination in the early hours of the morning. Too tired even to make up beds and go to bed, we sat outside by her pool. It was a hot sultry night and we opened a bottle of wine. Suddenly the conversation took an unexpected turn. She revealed that she had been adopted and had recently accessed her birth records. I was astounded, someone was actually admitting to being adopted. Here I was, at long last talking about this taboo subject to a relative stranger. That night was where the rest of my life started. She told me exactly what I had to do start the process and two months later I was sitting in the office of a kind and friendly social worker, looking at my actual birth certificate and my adoption papers. Those adoption papers revealed that I was the youngest of seven children. The next step, the social worker explained, was up to me if I wanted to try to track down those siblings. So, a few days later, armed with notebook and pen I arrived at Bedford Library, ready to wade through miles of microfiche records.

Several hours and a massive headache later, I'd discovered that I had three brothers and three sisters, and one of those sisters was called Judy, like me.

Having got so far, I did nothing for several years. The social worker had told me that the next step would be to try to locate some of these siblings. We'd already accessed the death certificates of my birth parents so I knew my siblings were the only people left who could throw light upon why I was adopted. Did I really want to meet these people and would they even know about me? Maybe they'd been told I'd died at birth. Maybe they knew about me but didn't want anything to do with me. Fear of rejection for a second time was also an issue in my mind. Could I cope with all the angst and emotion such reunions might cause. What if they were horrible people who once having met me would make my life a misery, what if this and what if ... My husband supported me but told me I'd made my own little family, but selfishly I thought that wasn't enough. Ultimately it had to be my decision and so I procrastinated.

Eventually, with much trepidation, I instigated the step into the unknown. The social worker located the address of one of my nephews and wrote to him. He straightaway contacted the sister who shared my name, and she rang my social worker, who then rang me. The final step of the whole, long process was about to begin, but not before I was to receive another shock. I was half suspecting that there would be another bombshell, and there was.

I was not the youngest of seven siblings. After I was adopted, my birth parents went on to have another baby, my younger sister, and she lived in the next village, ten minutes' drive away from me. So many emotions surfaced. Why had my birth parents given me away and then gone on to have another baby? My adoption papers had stated as reason for adoption, that with six children already, my birth parents couldn't afford to keep me. If that was true, why have another baby? They kept her, why, was she nicer than me? Those feelings of rejection surfaced again and I began to feel sorry for myself.

Then, I began to feel happier. Judy, my sister, had written a wonderful letter to me and had spoken warmly to me on the phone, but still the doubts were there. Was she just telling me what she thought I would want to hear, would I ever get the truth from anyone? Pushing my doubts aside, I decided to go ahead, the time had come to meet one of my sisters, the one who shared my name, the one, who I now knew, was at the High School with me, all those years ago, who had known that I was her sister and who had smiled warmly at me in those echoing corridors.

We arranged a meeting for the following Monday morning. All weekend I was unable to concentrate on anything. I was excited and terrified. What if she didn't like me or I took an instant dislike to her? How could I wriggle out of all this now it had started? What should I wear, what if there were long silences, what if we had nothing in common, what if..?

I crossed the road and there she was, my sister. We gave each other a hug and walked down the High Street, to the warmth of a small cafe where we talked non stop for about three hours. The photos came out and it was as if we had known each other all our lives. The friendly waitress took our photograph and we drank several cups of coffee.

I learned such a lot that day. The sadness of just missing meeting my brothers because I had waited so long before taking that final step. The joy of knowing that my siblings had known about me. The excitement when I was told that my oldest sister, who had lived in America most of her adult life, was coming over to England especially to meet me the following month, and the mixed emotions of learning about their childhood and some of the consequences that my own birth had had on all their lives. And, of course, I learned much about my birth parents, but that is another story and one that Judy must tell.

A month later, I met my oldest sister – my 'American' sister, Shirley. We all met in the same café where I had made my first sibling contact with Judy. It was such a happy occasion and I was made to feel so wanted. That dreadful fear of the unknown had now abated.

A few months after that, Jill, another 'American' sister, also came over to England, with her husband to meet me. Again we all met in that same café which had already seen two emotional reunions. Another happy occasion, and we all talked non-stop before I had to rush off to work, but not before arranging to meet a second time at my house.

In the meantime I made contact with my younger sister. It was also with mixed emotions that I set off to meet yet another new sibling and this time at a Garden Centre local to both of us. I need not have worried as we also talked for some time. I had now made contact with all my sisters.

That first Christmas of becoming a sister was full of joy. My mantelpiece proudly displayed Christmas cards with greetings that had never been seen in my house before – 'To my sister.' My lifelong secret was now out in the open.

I was amazed and humbled by the reaction from close friends when I'd first told them my news. Of course, they'd not known I was adopted or had suspected that I was either. I'd had years of practice at keeping my secret and had kept it well. Two of my oldest friends actually cried when they heard my story and my oldest friend that I'd known since Junior school days wrote me a heart-warming, long letter which made me cry too. I realised now that although I hadn't known my siblings all my life, I'd not been on my own through those lonely childhood years because I'd been so fortunate having such loving friends beside me.

It had taken me over sixty years finally to find my identity and my birth family. I cannot tell you the end of the story because it is still continuing and hopefully, will do so for many years to come. Our sibling relationships are still evolving. We were all victims of circumstances beyond our control. I feel so lucky and privileged to have been able to find my sisters, and my only regret is that I wasted so much time and didn't start looking for them earlier. My life now has a new dimension, for which I shall always be grateful.

Lightning Source UK Ltd.
Milton Keynes UK
UKOW03f1203120217
294173UK00001B/11/P